# LOSS, PAIN, AND FINDING PEACE

Shay_Marjanae

**LOSS, PAIN, AND FINDING PEACE**
Copyright © 2023 Shay_Marjanae
All rights reserved.

The author has shared her true story to the best of her recollection. For privacy reasons, some names, locations, and dates may have been changed.

Printed in the United States of America

ISBN: 978-1-953497-58-1 (Paperback)
ISBN: 978-1-953497-59-8 (Digital)

Library of Congress Control Number: 2023908342

Published by Cocoon to Wings Publishing
7810 Gall Blvd, #311
Zephyrhills, FL 33541
www.CocoontoWingsBooks.com
(813) 906-WING (9464)
Book design by ETP Creative

# LOSS, PAIN, AND FINDING PEACE

Cocoon to Wings
PUBLISHING

# DEDICATION

I dedicate this book, above all others, to my most Heavenly Father, my Big Daddy, my Best Friend, my Confidante, my Resting Place—God All-mighty. Without Him, I am nothing. Even when I didn't feel Him, He was there, walking with me. He is my strength. When I walked away from Him, He stayed with me and protected me. I dedicate not only this book, but my life, to Him.

I also dedicate this book to my family. To my husband, the man that came into my life and helped mold me into the woman that I am today—thank you. Through it all I know that you and our marriage were God's plan for my life. I love you. Thank you for loving me when I was unlovable. To the best children a mother could ever ask for, thank you for always trusting my decisions for you and allowing me to lead you as a mother should. Everyday wasn't sunshine, but we always found light. I love you to life; never forget that.

I would like to dedicate this book to the strongest and most beautiful woman that I know—my mother. Ma, thanks for everything. If we had to do it all over again, I would not change anything. Thank you for your honesty, always, even when it hurt, and I didn't agree. Thanks for loving me despite it all. You showed me God's love for me when I couldn't identify it. You are amazing and I'm proud to say that we are mother and daughter by chance, but friends by choice. Thanks for choosing me as a friend.

To the other four important men in my life: my dad (Derek Bell), my big brother (Willie Davis), my baby brother (De'Mario Walker, Sr.), and my uncle/Pastor (Eugene Davis, Jr.)—thank you for your protection and guidance.

# CONTENTS

*Dedication* ................................................................................................ iv

*Introduction* ............................................................................................ ix

When He Left                                                       1
(I Thought He Was My Superhero)

Daddy's World                                                      5

The Stepmother Fracture                                            9
(I Had To Meet The Standard)

The Day My Superhero Turned Into                                  13
The Villain (The Father Fracture)

Child-Sized Masks                                                 19

Mommy's World                                                     21

Don't Miss The Cues!                                             33

Masking To Survive                                               39

Searching For What's Missing                                     53

Trying To Find My Way (Where Is He?)     123

Love Is Blind     145

This Isn't Enough (But He Kept Me)     171

My Greatest Loss     183

Forgiveness (Unmasking)     229

It's Ugly!     241

Working Toward Greatness     247

Trust The Process!     283

How My Journey Ended     301

God's Promises To You     307

# INTRODUCTION

Loss, pain, and finding peace is my life. It has taken me a couple of years to write this book, mainly because I didn't want to face the uncertainty of emotions that come with telling my story. With all hesitation for telling my truth I didn't know telling my story was the start of a healing journey. The first couple of times I attempted to write, I hid behind all the good and what I thought you all would want to hear to make you feel good. I was afraid to write about some of the darkest times in my life, so I initially left those out. That was my way of telling the story without revealing my whole truth. Funny thing about writing about yourself is, you get to control the narrative. Well, at least that's what I thought. When you are following God's orders, things go in a totally different direction than where you think they should go. There were places I begged not to revisit, and God said, "Let's go there." There were times I cried, and I felt like this whole thing was stupid. There were times

I was so angry that I wanted to throw my computer and never pick it up again. But there were also times I laughed until I cried from some of the silly things I did. See, emotions were something that I built a wall around and I wasn't used to feeling anymore. You will find out why as you read. I hope this book helps you identify where you left yourself during trauma and how to start the healing process. There is life after trauma, but it takes work to get there. Grab yourself a few tissues; you might need them, and let's dive in.

# WHEN HE LEFT
## (I thought he was my Superhero)

It amuses me when adults think that young children don't remember the things that took place around them and the things that happened to them.

Go with me as I revisit the places and things that shaped me into who I am today and take away from this the lessons you need to be set free.

**** 

BOOM! That was the sound of the door meeting the frame as it slammed. I jumped and it made my heart start to race. I moved closer to my big brother on the couch, the vibration of the door filled my little body with fear. I heard my mother screaming; she was crying as she pleaded for it to stop, running from room to room trying to get away from him. The monster was attacking my mother. My brother and I moved into a corner of the hallway for safety as we sat in the nook of the corner with our backs against the cold, freshly painted white wall. He held me tight in his four-year-old arms. I started to cry as I clutched the brown carpet in between my tiny fingers to find extra security. I was so afraid; I knew that I had better be still and quiet. I didn't want whatever was getting my mother to get me. I wasn't sure of what was happening. But I knew it wasn't good. When the monster busted out the room, I looked, and it was my dad. The expression on his face reminded me of The Incredible Hulk, the 70's character who turned green, grew big, and popped out of his clothes when he got angry. He stomped out, looked down on us huddled in the corner of the hallway. He asked with a frown, "Are you going with me or staying with your momma?"

His tone made me clam up and move a little closer to my brother. I turned and looked to my brother for his reply. He said, "Staying." I followed his lead. My dad was a big man. He stood six feet two inches tall with his dark chocolate skin and, if I had to guess, he was 235 pounds back then. My father turned away and aggressively walked out of the house in a rage, slamming the door behind him. We remained seated in the cold corner as we listened to our mother weep. We wanted to go to her aid, but we were afraid to move. Now, my mom was a petite woman. My mom is light-skinned, and she stands only five feet tall and, back then, maybe 145 pounds. She was no competition for my dad.

Shortly after he stormed out of the house, the car door slammed and the next sound we heard were tires screeching loudly down the road. My brother held me a little tighter because I was shaking out of fear. It was the loudest noise I had ever heard. I held my brother tight clutching his shirt in my hand because if he moved, I was moving too. There was the usual feeling in my chest, something was thumping fast and hard. I looked down at my shirt to see nothing out of the ordinary. My breaths became short and shallow, it was hard to breath, so I held my breath and waited for the sound to vanish. Even as I write this book, if I hear tires screeching, I grow nervous and anxious. But the plot thickens.

# DADDY'S WORLD

> *Between two and seven years old, the rabbit hole got deeper and darker.*

After the big blow up, my dad moved out and my parents split time with us. We would spend time with him on the weekends. He was my BEST friend. The best times were when I was about four. He and I spent time alone doing things that I liked. One of my favorite things was to go out to eat. We would talk and talk. Even at age four, they were convinced that I would be a lawyer because I loved to talk and debate about everything, I was able to hold full conversations. I had been talking since I was about nine months, according to my mom. My dad made me feel important, he listened to every word and asked questions; he would even inquire about the names of my friends. He taught me my right from my left. This was important to him, he wanted to make sure that I used the right hand, but I'm left-handed and he didn't like that; I believe because it made me different. No one else in the immediate family was left-handed. So how did it happen to me as if it was a disease or something? He didn't like that I was left-handed, but I was a left-handed thumb sucker. He tried everything to get me to stop sucking my thumb. He wrapped it up, only for me to sneak and unwrap it in a hiding place. He put hot sauce and all kinds of different things I didn't like on my thumb to keep me from sucking it. But I would just go into the bathroom and wash it off. I would get a spanking, but the comfort and safety my thumb provided me was worth the spanking. It was like a security blanket that I took with me everywhere. When I got older, I inquired how I became a left-handed thumb sucker, and I learned that I didn't start sucking my thumb until I was two years old. That's when he left! However, my dad was my superhero. I had another favorite thing—going street racing with him and his friends. That was the best thing ever! Although the tires screeched, I made sure that I was standing so close to my brother or dad that I became a piece of their clothing because my heart would beat so fast, and I needed to hide my face and hold on to them tight until that part was over. I was always excited to see the cars go so fast. They all had Mustangs; there were black, green, white, yellow, blue ones. I believe there was one like "The Dukes of Hazzard" car. "The Dukes of Hazzard" was a 1979 comedy sitcom. I remembered my dad having a dark-colored one that I thought was the greatest car ever! I watched him work on it weekend after weekend, under the carport, if he wasn't racing it. The fast and the furious started way before the movie series. I would sometimes lay next to him, on the ground, underneath the car to see what he was doing. He took pride in that car.

On race day, my dad would sometimes sit me on the roof of his car with a towel to protect my legs from the hot roof as his friends raced up and down the street. It was exciting to watch and to see the smile on his face. He was happy. And when there was a smile, I believed the monster that I knew was gone. But I was always cautious not to anger him because I didn't know when or if the monster would appear. I was happy when I was with him, despite how he treated my mother and how he had abandoned his family.

My family used to say that I was a carbon copy of my dad. I must admit that I have a few characteristics of his. He loves music and so do I. I used to sit with him for hours listening to music in the living room of his house, we would listen to all types of music. He had crates and crates of albums. If you are an early 80's baby or older, then you remember albums. Although they are making a comeback. He listened through his big, black, over-the-ear headphones that he plugged into the stereo. He would lay on his back, on the carpeted floor, with his headphones on, staring at the ceiling, I would crawl on him and put my head on his chest and listen to his heartbeat. Our hearts would beat in rhythm together and I thought those moments would last forever. It was just me and my superhero. On those days, I thought I would be his baby forever. That dream quickly tarnished.

# THE STEPMOTHER FRACTURE
## (I Had To Meet The Standard)

By the time I was six years old, it was normal for me to be left with my pregnant stepmom. When my dad went car racing or to hang out, he only took my brother. Things started going downhill from there. The rabbit hole started to open. I was no longer excited to go to my dad's house; but I would go because I was hoping that we would spend some time together. Yet, spending time with him happened less and less as each weekend came and passed by.

Going places with my stepmom required a certain standard, and my mom wasn't meeting those standards when she would send us over for the weekend. Because of this, my stepmom used to take me to the "Family Dollar" Store to buy clothes for me and while doing so, she spoke badly about my mother as if I didn't understand. My father was well employed and so was she, so to buy me clothes from "Family Dollar" reinforced to me that she didn't care about me. After purchasing the clothes, we would go back to the house and get dressed before going to her mom's house.

> ## "I Hated Going To Her Mother's House."

It was such a bittersweet experience because playing with the kids at my step-grandmother's house allowed me to escape my situation. Still, I hated going there because those women would talk about me as if I didn't understand because I was young. Once, they spent quite some time talking about how ugly and black I was right in front of me as if I wasn't there. I continued to sit on the hard, worn brown carpet and played with the dolls pretending I didn't hear or understand. I tried to block it out, but I couldn't block out the agony I felt on the inside. I tried to build walls around me to protect me from their words, but they still somehow seemed to seep in. The walls I was trying to build were the invisible ones that only you can see and feel, but with each word they spoke, a brick was removed from my wall. It felt like I was suffocating. I tried to shrink inside myself to hide within while still being visible. I created so much noise in my head to drown out the things that were being said about me and I refused to let them see me cry. But I questioned if my mother and family lied to me. They always told me how pretty I was, and how I had the prettiest complexion. I mean one of my aunts used to and still calls me "chocolate" because my skin was dark and smooth. This was a conversation that happened on more than one occasion. I never told my mother because I loved my dad, and I didn't want to do anything to jeopardize that or diminish my time with him. But being called "black" and "ugly" by adults killed my self-esteem at an early age.

> *I believed the lies of the enemy.*

No matter how pretty my family told me I was, all I heard in my head was, "Her black a** with them buck teeth. I don't know why her mammy let her suck her thumb."

Do you know it only takes one negative comment to erase every positive thing you have ever heard?

# THE DAY MY SUPERHERO TURNED INTO THE VILLAIN

## (The Father Fracture)

I wanted to go over to my dad's house less and less. My last visit left a dark mark on my heart. We were sitting at the dinner table - my dad, my stepmom, my brother, and stepbrother, and me. As we were preparing to eat, my stepmom leaned over and said something to my dad in his ear. To this day I don't know what she said. Whatever she said to him made him look at me with disgust.

The room grew cold, and I sunk in my chair, my stomach started to feel queasy from the smell and look of the food. I saw the monster appearing by the daunting look in his eyes and the scowl on his face. As he stared at me, I felt all the little power I had shattering with each second, I was shrinking. It seemed like the more she talked the darker his eyes became. When she was done, he looked at me and said, "I am going to whoop yo' a**!" The tears started streaming down my face because I didn't know what I had done that disappointed him so much. Then he demanded from me, "So, you're hunching toys?" I had no idea what he was talking about. I had never heard that word before. I wasn't sure what he was talking about, but from the tone in his voice, I knew I was in trouble. Fear choked me and I couldn't say a word. I parted my lips to answer, but nothing would come out. He asked the question again and sound escaped me. I couldn't say a word. I was confused about what to say. I tried to utter words the second time he asked, but all I could do was shrug my shoulders. Fear had robbed me of my voice, but I knew I had better say something or make a gesture because the silence and tears appeared to him like I was guilty when it was my sheer confusion as to what he meant.

I don't know why he whooped me. That whooping quickly divided the bond between my dad and me. At that point, I didn't want to ever go back to their house because I knew she hated me. The other times I was spanked I understood why, but that time I wasn't sure, and my heart was shattered. My superhero had created me to be the villain. That was a hurt I couldn't show or explain.

That next day was daunting, and I counted down the shades of the sky until it was time to go home. I don't think I said five words that day. I felt as if I didn't have purpose; the monster had taken all the happiness that I had in me. I finally understood what happened to my mom that night he left us. I didn't feel important to him anymore; he stole my joy. I was broken. I wanted to go home to my momma.

When it was time to go home, I didn't tell his family goodbye; I left with half a wave to them. I sat quiet the whole ride home. When he pulled up to my house, I held my tears because I wanted to tell him how much he hurt me, and I didn't like him anymore. He let me out the back seat. I walked toward the house with my head held high without looking back. He said, "Bye, Blacky." That was his nickname for me. I walked into my mother's house, and I never parted my lips to say anything.

I was excited to see my mom because I survived the monster just like she did, so I felt a bit closer to her. I talked to her like nothing had ever happened. It was dark when we got home so there wasn't much time before getting prepared for the week. I took a bath and did some self-talk telling myself I never wanted to see him again, and that night began my hatred toward my stepmom.

After bathing, I went to bed as agony filled up my entire being. If I was a balloon, I would have popped by the slightest touch. But I knew that I had to keep it together a little longer. Still, the minute I laid down, and buried my face in the pillow, I cried. I felt like a part of me had been snatched away without warning. That was the last time I was at his house. At that point, I was so hurt I didn't care if I ever saw him again.

As I look back on this chapter of my life, I understand where the seeds of abandonment, rejection, and fear were planted. Masks were also birthed in that season. So, when he left, I was left with seeds that I didn't know would not only go with me but grow with me.

# Reflection

I would like for you to take a minute and reflect on any of the points in your life where you felt fear, abandonment, and rejection. Using the questions provided, write about it in this Reflection section.

*What seeds do you possess?*
*Who in your childhood do you need to release?*
*What negative thing was spoken over you that you need to return to its rightful owner?*
*Do you remember a time fear stole your voice?*

_____

_____

_____

_____

_____

_____

_____

_____

_____

_____

_____

# Reflection

_____

_____

_____

_____

_____

_____

_____

_____

_____

_____

_____

_____

_____

_____

_____

_____

_____

# CHILD-SIZED MASKS

Children learn to wear masks at young ages.

That last visit with my dad taught me how to mask, hide, and cover everything up. On the ride home, there was background noise, but for me it was more of an awkward silence. I sat in that moment with the wind blowing gracefully in my face as I sat in the back seat, alone. I simply stared at the back of the driver's seat. I contemplated how to, or if I should, tell my mom what happened. When my dad, brother, and I arrived in that moment, I knew that I should pretend that I was ok. That was my first time purposely putting on my mask.

From the ages of two until seven I learned to adjust and switch masks to the changes of our normal in life.

Although I missed him a lot, I learned to live without my dad. I didn't want my mom to know, so

I didn't bring him up much. When I did, I saw the look on her face that I can now identify as hurt and disappointment. That was an indicator for me that it wasn't the day to talk about him.

# MOMMY'S WORLD

> *Mom made the best of our time together.*

We didn't have much; my mom was a stay-at-home welfare mom. It was easier for her, and she did the best she could by us. We didn't have a car, so our adventures were right on the other side of the door. I believe her favorite thing was spending time with us.

On Saturday mornings, after cartoons and cereal, Ma would get us dressed to go outside. On the prettiest sunny days, she would ask, "What are you cooking today?" She knew that entertained my imagination. I couldn't wait to get outside to show her that I could cook, just like her. I was a baby chef, cooking with my kitchen set. I cooked leaves, sticks, dirt, added a little water as I sat in the middle of the front yard. The sun would kiss my skin ever so gently; and, the wind would blow ever so slightly, cooling the sweat on my little forehead as I worked hard to prepare my dinner. I explored the outside, searching for all my ingredients while she sat with friends on the porch. I made collard greens, fried chicken, rice, and cornbread. I would take her the food I prepared on a nice little pink plate. She would pretend to eat it and tell me how yummy it was. I smile now because I can visualize the moment. I didn't always cook the same thing; I had a menu.

My mom and I were so in tune with one another. I used to watch my mom's face and her expressions would signal how I should respond. If I should give her a hug, a smile, or just leave her alone because she was fine. Now I understand that things were a little rough for her. We didn't go to church, but I believe that my momma talked to God all the time. She didn't know much to teach us when it came to Faith, but my momma made us say "The Lord's Prayer" every night. We would kneel on the side of the bed, and she said, "Repeat after me. 'Our Father who art in heaven hallowed be thy name. Thy kingdom come; thy will be done on earth as it is in heaven.'" (Matthew 6:9-13). I had no idea what I prayed; I didn't even know what I asked God to do for me. I was following mom's lead.

No matter how good things were, I loved and missed my dad.

I had Frank, my stepdad, who came into my life at about a year after my dad left. Frank loved me dearly, but it didn't feel the same as my father's love. What I understand now is that I built a wall so that he couldn't take my dad's place. I didn't realize it until I was seven that he loved me as his own.

Frank wasn't a very big man like my dad. But he was a protector. I didn't fear the monster returning when he was there. The cool thing was Frank was an 18-wheeler truck driver, so we were always traveling. When my brother and I had long weekends or vacations from school, we went on road trips. He did everything to make us feel as if he was our biological father, and although he was the father figure in my life, I missed my daddy like crazy. Over time, I learned to be okay with it. That's when the masks started to appear regularly.

*Did you know that kids can wear masks too?*

Early in my life I cared about the feelings of other people. My stepfather was there for us, so I pretended that I loved my stepdad as much as I loved my dad. But deep down on the inside, I wanted my dad.

I dreamt about my dad most nights and that was the extent of our relationship. In my mind, I was Daddy's little girl. Those dreams were so real to me.

We always did something I loved like going to the park, skating rink, bowling, and even drag racing. I would wake up with so much happiness in my heart; until I realized that it was all a dream.

Seven was a significant age for me. I was the youngest child until then; that's when my baby brother was born, and things changed for me. I thought my mother wasn't going to have time for me. Everyone came over to see the baby. Who was going to see about me?

Before my brother was born, I used to sit on my momma's lap all the time. But when my brother came along, she was always holding him; her lap didn't have room for me any longer. I didn't understand. I used to ask myself, "Where am I supposed to sit now?" I would cry when I wasn't able to sit on her lap. That was my place of security. That was my assurance that she still wanted me. Even then, God was there. God knew what I needed as a broken little girl. He knew that I needed to see and feel love. He gave me the best godparents that any child could ever ask for.

One day we had family over and everyone was concerned about whether the baby opened his eyes yet. I felt invisible because no one checked on me. One day, I must have had a sad look on my face because my godmother said, "Come here. I will hold you."

And she did. That was security for me, security that I really needed. That was God's way of keeping me and comforting me. I went back to being content with life. I was in a place where things felt almost normal.

Once I got used to having my godmother's lap, another bombshell was dropped. She was having a baby. I was starting to feel like I wasn't going to have a place in her life either. I learned that I had to pretend to be something I was not. I learned to pretend that I was happy and that everything was fine. My dad left me, now my mom had a new love, and my godmother was having a baby. I didn't understand then that a parent loves all their children the same. I tried everything to be seen; but I still felt invisible. I understand now that nothing or no one can compete with a newborn baby! Their smell, their cry, their stretch, just everything about them makes your heart melt.

At eight years old, I thought that my mom didn't want me, and my baby brother didn't want to connect with me either. A year passed; and he only played with my older brother, but not with me. I thought that something was wrong with me. I pretended that I was okay with that, too. Every night I still said The Lord's Prayer because it was routine. I questioned what was and who was this "OUR FATHER." He was not my father; nobody wanted to be my daddy. And all the while, God wanted to be my daddy; I just didn't know that. He wanted to fill the void, but I didn't know how to let Him at that age. The seed of rejection was growing. But as I prayed to Him, there was something about it that gave me a feeling I couldn't explain. After I said The Lord's Prayer, I felt like a sense of relief, and took a deep sigh, just knowing within that everything was going to be okay. But somehow, I still felt unwanted.

At the time, we weren't living in the best of situations. Since I had learned to be okay with everything, even the conditions we lived in at the time were fine with me. It was not easy, but we made it work.

One day we had a family gathering when we were living in low-income housing, which we called "the projects." That day, my mom and older cousin were leaving. I wasn't sure where they were going but I wanted to go, too. My mom didn't allow me to go. I was upset, but I soon got over it. Later, I was playing outside around dusk. I saw my mom walking down the street. I was puzzled as to why she was walking because she had left with our cousin in his truck. It was clear that something was wrong. She kept looking back as if someone was following her. She got to the porch where my uncles and other adult cousins were waiting. She was dirty, like she had been wrestling in the dirt, and hysterical. All the adults were attentive to her. They were checking her face and body for wounds. She proceeded to tell them how they were robbed. I didn't know what that meant, but I knew that it was bad. I asked her, "Where is Louis?" He is the cousin she left with. She said that they let her go and that the robbers hit him in the head with a gun. She thought they were going to kill him.

As the adult family members prepared to go to where Louis and my mom had been, Louis pulled up in his white truck. He was bleeding from somewhere, but I couldn't tell where from. I was so scared. I silently cried that night as I laid in my bed. I thought that the people who robbed my momma were going to get us. I believed they knew where we lived.

Life kept happening and things were as we knew them. Now, if you've never been to or seen the projects, they are typically large two-story block buildings placed in rows on several connecting streets. We lived on the first row, closest to the main street. Across the street from our project was "Belmont Heights" Little League Baseball Park. My older brother and my little cousin, Julius, played baseball at the park and my mom, brothers, and I would walk over to watch. One Saturday, Julius had a game, but my brother didn't, so we didn't go to the park. We stayed home and sat on the porch, simply watching things happening in the neighborhood. There were always things happening in the projects and you learned how to stay safe and not react to it. We saw riots, robberies, fights, all kinds of stuff. This was normal there. However, out of all the things I saw living in the projects, I had never seen, in person, a dead body. Unfortunately, the first time I saw one, it was someone that I knew.

As we sat on the porch, Mom was talking to the neighbor and the kids were playing. We started to hear a lot of commotion and people screaming. The sirens started coming from every direction. When Julius' baseball game was over, Judy, Julius' mom, came over. She was pregnant with my cousin, Angelo, at the time. My mom and Judy were favorite cousins, so it was customary for them to come over after a game. When she got by us, she asked my mom whether she heard anything about what happened. She told my mom, "I could hear the sirens at the park."

Mom replied, "I'm not sure what happened."

They told me to go and see what happened. I begged them not to make me go. I was scared.

Judy said, "Girl, go see what happened."

Reluctantly, I grabbed my friend and went to see what was going on. The commotion had happened two rows back. I peeped around the corner, and I saw people standing outside, watching the police as they did their work. There were a lot of police officers. I stepped out, but I stood at the corner of the building, observing. As I looked around, I saw the police officers were putting sheets on the people who were laying down. I initially couldn't understand what was happening. I wondered why they were covering them. Were they cold? I watched the police more closely because they were going from person to person and lifting the sheet and putting it back down. There was a body lying on the ground, there was one laying in the doorway, and there was one in the driver's seat of a car. They all had sheets over them. I was still standing at the corner when the last police officer was lifting the sheets and writing things down. I noticed that these men weren't moving, no matter what was happening to them. The police came over to the car where the last body was, the door was open. The police leaned in, and he looked. The person's head was leaned back on the headrest. I watched closely because I knew that I had to go back and report what happened. The police pulled the sheet off the head of the person, and all the air escaped my body. It was Big Angelo. I stared to see if he was going to move or if he was breathing. My heart was beating fast. I didn't know what to think. There was blood streaming down his face, but his eyes were open. I didn't know whether he was dead or alive. I was scared. I watched as the officer took his two fingers and closed his eyes. He didn't move. At that point, I knew he was dead. I didn't know what I was going to say when I got back home. I started to cry because I knew that I had to tell Judy what I saw. I wanted to be brave (mask), so I gathered my eight-year-old self and walked back to my house. My mom and Judy were sitting on the porch. I made sure to have no evidence of tears.

In unison, they asked me, "What happened?"

I looked at them and with slight hesitation I responded, "Angelo's dead." I would never forget the look on their faces.

With disbelief, Judy screamed, "WHAT?"

I said, "Angelo dead in a car."

She took off from the porch crying and holding her stomach and my mom ran behind her. When we all returned to the scene and she saw him, she was hysterical. Judy begged the police officers to allow her to get closer. My mom and her went over to the car. She grabbed her stomach as she slowly fell to the ground weeping. My mom fell to the ground with her, and they both cried. I watched from the corner of the building. I didn't quite understand death, but I knew that his death caused her extreme hurt from the way she cried. I had nightmares for weeks. I dealt with it by pretending that it didn't happen.

I developed a mask for every situation. Masking was a coping mechanism that I used. I would say I was okay when I was crying on the inside, smiling, when I wanted to scream. Do those masks sound familiar? It's easy to miss masks in children, but you can see them by looking for behavioral changes in them. Sometimes these changes would be due to some type of trauma that has occurred in the child's life, like it was for me.

I got to the point where being in my bedroom was the only place I wanted to be. That's where I was able to shut out the world. There were no dead bodies, no robberies, no baby brothers, no stepdads. It was just me and my baby dolls.

When I became a parent, I didn't want to miss the signs with my children, nieces, or nephews, so I paid close attention to them. Considering everything I had walked through, up until the point of Angelo's death, I hid my emotional scars under the "I'm happy" mask, the "I'm good" mask, the "Nothing's wrong" mask.

# DON'T MISS THE CUES!

As a child, no one paid attention to the masks I wore. The masks were as invisible as I felt back then. I believe kids today will mask through music and social media. By paying attention to the music they listen to and the things they post on their socials, one could detect the masks. I know with my own children I could tell what kind of day they were having because of the music they were listening to. This told me if they were happy, sad, angry, or feeling defeated. Either way, it opened the door for conversation. For me, it was their cry for help. I used to miss all the signs until I started paying attention. I wasn't having conversations because I thought that they were just listening to music until I noticed the pattern. One thing I'm learning as a parent is children will talk if we take the time to listen. I wanted someone to listen to me as a child, that's why I make it my mission at this stage in life to pay close attention to the signals kids give off.

It is important to pay attention to behaviors as mentioned because behaviors change. However, be careful how you approach the situation because you don't want the child to shut down or feel uncomfortable. Take a moment and remember when you were their age. Sometimes sharing a memory with them about when you were their age and what happened with you helps them to remain open. I believe our children need to know that we are human, and things happened to us, and we survived. This is what I believe will allow children to shed their "I'm okay" mask and tell you what's bothering them. I notice that kids also mask to meet the parent's caliber. I had a friend who was a different person when she was at my house than when she was at her home. I asked her one day why she was so different when she came over, and she looked at me with tears in her eyes and said, "My mom would never understand me."

I could not let that happen to my own kids. They will tell you to this day that I watched them like a hawk, but it was necessary to ensure they understood it was okay to talk about their feelings and not hide them. I only wished someone had done that for me earlier in my life. If someone would have studied me, they would have noticed the behavior changes.

I would have lived a different life instead of finding new masks. I would have never gotten comfortable with wearing them. Now, I am an advocate for counseling. I believe if I would have had someone to talk to and work through things, I wouldn't have carried the trauma from decade to decade.

I believe that children should go to counseling. When I was younger, and in my culture, counseling wasn't something you did. You kept it in and rolled with the punches. It's important for us to make counseling normal. It would have saved me the years of distress I spent trying to save myself.

# Reflection

When I start to reflect on this season of my life, I seek to heal in the areas of trauma. But a friend of mine helped me to understand that, although we have removed our child-size masks, the residue is still present. I learned in this healing process that when removing an uncomfortable child-size mask as an adult, it takes work to remove the residue. You know when something has been in place a long time, there is always residue. Imagine a picture that has been in the same place for decades and everything around it has changed. When you remove that picture because it no longer goes with your décor of your home you notice that the wall behind it is a different color than the rest of the wall. You notice the thick dust behind the frame, you notice that the picture no longer serves a purpose, but it needs to be cleaned. That's healing and deliverance. While healing, don't forget to clean the residue.

What child-sized masks are you still in possession of? Have you removed the residue?

_____

_____

_____

# Reflection

_____

_____

_____

_____

_____

_____

_____

_____

_____

_____

_____

_____

_____

_____

_____

_____

_____

_____

_____

_____

# Reflection

_____

_____

_____

_____

_____

_____

_____

_____

_____

_____

_____

_____

_____

_____

_____

_____

_____

_____

# MASKING TO SURVIVE

I was the youngest of my cousins who hung out together. Because of this I wanted to make myself noticeable. I knew that I was great at dancing, so I used that to get attention. I tried to learn every dance. My brother and I would get on the dance floor almost immediately after the music started. The adults would call for us to come dance. There was one party, when everyone was dancing; I sat to the side and watched.

My uncle said to me, "Come on, get on the dance floor."

With the biggest smile, I rushed to the dance floor to show off my moves. It became a dance challenge between my uncle and me. I did all the latest dances. I knew for sure that I would out-dance him. By the end of the third song, he smiled and said, "You are my dance partner from now on."

I was excited because I mattered. The seed of abandonment was put on hold. It wasn't growing as rapidly because someone wanted me.

By the middle of my third-grade year, I was enrolled in Edison Elementary. My first teacher there was Ms. Chandler. I walked with her to pick up the other kids from physical education. They were all lined up and as they walked by us, they stared at me. I was scared. I made sure that I had on my best masks. The masks of confidence, happiness, and security. But, as each student walked by, I felt myself sinking because I was none of those things. See, the funny thing about masks is they are always what we are not but want to be. And somehow, we convince ourselves that it's a pass. No one said anything, they just looked at me.

Then, toward the end of the line, there was a boy that said, "Hey!" I gave a slight wave, holding my breath, trying to control my breathing. He said, "What's your name?"

I took a breath and said, "Shayorka," while trying to withhold all the nervousness I felt. I felt as if I was shaking like a leaf.

He asked, "Huh?"

I understood because I don't have a common name.

I felt like they were going to make fun of my name. I didn't repeat myself I just continued to walk with the teacher. When we got to the class, I was hoping that she placed me in the back of the room, in a corner, next to a window. There I could be invisible since all my masks had fallen off. Oh, how I was so wrong. I was seated right smack dab in the middle of the class. I thought to myself, PERFECT! I hurried and got myself together. As I fumbled through my imaginary mask, I put on my favorite mask; the "everything is okay" mask. It seemed like once I gathered myself, the teacher called my name, and she MESSED IT UP and the giggles started. I questioned myself as to why my mom gave me this name. My eyes filled with tears, but I refused to let a tear drop. I thought no one would like me there either.

The rejection seed grew a little bit more. I started to dislike my name. I thought that I would never have friends. So, I only hung out with my cousins. That wasn't always fun either. One time, I was at a family function and the kids were swimming. I couldn't swim for nothing. My mom had put my brother and I in swimming lessons, but I couldn't grasp it. We were enjoying the pool. I don't know what I did to upset one of my cousins, but he was mad at me, I guessed. Everyone knew that I couldn't swim. I would get out of the pool at three feet and walk down to the other end to talk to my cousins. As I stood on the edge of the pool and talked to my favorite cousin, my cousin Darryl pushed me into six feet. In six feet of water! I thought I was going to die. Again, BUT GOD! As I sank to the bottom, I couldn't breathe, and I panicked. Thank God my other cousins were there. They heard the splash, but they didn't see me. The third time I came up for air, one of my cousins saw me. She tried to save me, but she couldn't do it alone. I was drowning fast. My other two cousins came to our aid because I was drowning her as she tried to save me; they saved our lives. I cried and thought my cousin hated me because he tried to kill me by throwing me into the deep end. I held on to that and didn't speak to him for many years after that. To this day, our relationship has never been the same. Yet, despite my near-death experience that day, I learned to swim.

I returned to school that Monday and, as the months went by, I gained friends, not just one or two, I had lots of friends. When the school year ended, I was a little sad because I thought I would lose all the friends I finally had. But when I found out that I was returning to Edison, I was excited. When I returned to school to start fourth grade, I had a teacher named Mrs. Worthtine. God bless her soul. That lady loved me! Again, God. God knew that I needed love, and it was still something I longed for. She taught with her heart, and she disciplined with love. She was the best. She did not only tell me that I was smart, but she also showed me that I was smart, and she made sure that there were ways I could succeed.

School was challenging for me. I struggled with reading. I never had a teacher that cared about me learning to read until Mrs. Worthtine. She did everything she could to make sure I succeeded. I used to stay after school with her, she provided extra help for me and a few others. For additional help, there was a reading teacher named Mrs. Boothe. She was about her business. She pulled me out of class to work with her and a group of kids, and it was a fun atmosphere. I didn't mind going to Reading because she believed in me. Things were good. I had friends, I was going to sleep overs and hanging out. Then, it was time to move. Things were financially hard for my family, and I was devastated. I thought, *Oh no! I'm going to lose my friend. What am I going to do?*

I had just made a new friend; she was a grade ahead of me. After weeks of panic, I learned that we were moving in with my aunt. I was extremely happy because my aunt lived directly behind the school. Now I could see my friends after school.

Before that summer came, I had a best friend. That was my first best friend since my dad. We would spend time together after school, write notes to one another and all the things little girls do.

When it was time for school to be out for the summer, because she was a grade ahead of me she was leaving the school. And I was leaving the neighborhood. On the last day of school, we cried and cried like it was the end of our friendship. I'm not sure why she cried, but I cried because I felt I was being abandoned by another best friend. We hugged and cried like the sisters on the movie, *The Color Purple*. We thought that we would never see each other again. As she started her journey in the sixth grade, and me the fifth, we remained friends. But as the year went on, the communication between us vanished. I had lost my best friend. There were other friends, but none of them were her. Fifth grade year was different without her.

It was time to move again. We moved into a new house that summer as I got ready to enter sixth grade. I shuffled through my feelings. Feelings of worry, hopelessness, loneliness, abandonment, rejection, and simply not being enough to make anyone I got close to stay in my life. Love still didn't look like it should to me. The seed of abandonment started to reign over all the other planted seeds. My thoughts assured me that we would never be stable. I would never have a dad in my life. The feeling of being an outcast was not okay. As I figured out how to house all these things within, I found my masks. I started to wear them again because I knew I had to adjust to the world around me and make new friends. Friends were important to me. They helped me escape the thoughts and the feelings that tormented me daily.

That summer I wondered what sixth grade would be like. I didn't give it too much thought because I knew that I would figure it out. My brother and I were signed up for the summer program at the local park. We had all kinds of activities, went on field trips, and did all types of things. It was a fun-filled summer until we went on a field trip to McFarland Park. That was a time where I can now see God was present. We got to the park, and there were obstacles everywhere. There were slip-and-slides, tug of war, mountain climbing, hula hoops, dodge ball, you name it, we had it there at the park. I went through a few of the games and obstacles. It was my turn to do the slip-and-slide. At McFarland Park there is this tall hill that seemed to me at that time to be the tallest hill I had ever seen. I climbed to the top of the tall, steep hill. When you reached the top, you would find a partner. I saw my brother, so I decided that was my partner. That was who I was going to race. I thought I had a good chance of being close behind him because I knew that I was going to lose. It was our turn and we got to the front of the line. I saw others do this, so, I was thinking *I got this,* although my heart was beating like a jackhammer from fear.

I looked down the slope to where I needed to end up and took a deep breath. My brother looked at me and said, "I'm not taking it easy on you." At that moment, all the fear left my body, and I was ready to prove to him that I didn't need him to take it easy on me. The coach said, "Y'all ready?" I stood in the running stance ready for him to say go. I wasn't scared, but my heart was beating fast. With the next deep breath, the whistle blew. We took off down the slippery slip-and-slide slope. I took about five good steps down the slope and my foot lost grip. I flew up in the air and fell on my back. The impact of the fall knocked all the air out of my lungs. I laid there a second and then jumped up because I remembered my brother saying he wasn't going to take it easy on me. I continued to run down the slope while gasping for air.

My eyes were huge, my mouth was wide open trying to get a fraction of air in my lungs. I couldn't breathe, but I kept running. All I could see was my brother ahead of me and not looking back. Once I reached the bottom of the hill, I fell to my knees, desperately trying to breathe. The impact was so hard that I couldn't get air to come into my lungs or go out. I was scared. I bent over, clutching myself. I wanted to cry, but I couldn't because I couldn't breathe. I started to get lightheaded, sound and vision were starting to fade. As I was blacking out, my brother came over and placed his hand on my back and asked, "Are you, okay?" At that very moment, it felt like all the wind in my lungs were restored and I started to cry. He went to get the counselor who waved for one of the paramedics and they came over and checked me out. I didn't have anything physically wrong with me; so, after checking me, they allowed me to sit out the rest of the time. As I think back that day could have had a different ending. But God!

After that summer, I went to Potter Middle School. It was for sixth graders only. I was nervous about starting, but on the first day I saw my friends from Edison. Then I was as happy as a kid in a candy store. School was fun! After school I went to my great grandmother's house, but I didn't like it. I never told my mother because I didn't want to switch schools.

Mom was a working/single parent, by this time her and Frank had separated, and the only way I was able to go to Potter was to go to my great grand-mother's house after school. I would arrive hungry and not be able to eat unless my grandmother was there. There were many days when my grandmother would return, or my mom would come to pick me up and I would be sitting on the porch, starving. I never told my mom what happened or how hungry I was because I didn't want her to ruffle any feathers that may have caused me to leave the school and my friends. Friends were everything to me. Friends allowed an escape. It was somewhere I didn't have to focus on my true feelings.

While attending Potter, I met new friends that I also connected with. By sixth grade I started answer-ing to the name Shay. My grandmother always called me Shay because she was unable to pronounce my name. Because Shay was common, this allowed me to feel normal as if I fit in and not like an outcast because no one had my name. I looked for many ways to connect and not seem too different than everyone else.

I met this girl named Cookie in physical education (PE) class. As we talked, we learned that we shared some of the same family members, so we instantly started calling one another cousins. I felt a sense of belonging. I had friends and a cousin at school. I thought that this was the best thing ever. I started to spend time with her and started to hang out at her house. We grew close, so by summer we were inseparable; we did everything together. Cookie had a friend named Crystal. As I got to know Crystal, I found out that we had some cousins in common. That was crazy; I now had two girl cousins my age.

There it was the three of us, but Cookie and I were together more often. Summer vacation was here, and we spent time together. Well, we did what we could. We mostly shopped and took pictures; we were at the mall every weekend. We started catching the city bus from her house to mine. We would have fun. On the bus ride, on the walk to and from the bus stop, we ALWAYS had a disposable camera. Therefore, we would stop on the sidewalk or street to take pictures. WE LOVED PICTURES!

I don't quite remember how it happened, but I had a boyfriend. At 12 I had a boyfriend, and his name was Sedrick. Sedrick was a bad boy; he was dark-skinned with his big eyes. He was the cutest; he puts me in the mind of the actor, Omar Epps. He was special to me; he was the first to love me outside of my family and he showed it the way he knew how as a young man.

Sitting in the middle of my bed as I write this, thinking back I smile because he made me feel special at such an early age. He always made sure I was okay by building me up, writing me love letters, telling me that he loved me. He would buy me things like teddy bears, sweet and salty snacks, you know, little things that he could afford. Remember earlier in the story when I shared about the boy at the end of the line when I was in the third grade? The one who was the first to say hi to me. Well, that was Sedrick. He was my friend first, and we always had fun together - you know the type of fun that we had in the 80s and 90s. Playing sand lock, racing, hide and seek, jungle gyms, monkey bars, getting wet in the sprinklers, climbing trees, jumping fences, playing tag, even drinking out of the water hose. That good ole days fun! It just happened that he became my very first boyfriend. From early on in our relationship, he would protect me and bought things for me. I think back on that now and it's funny that I always wanted and looked for protection. He was one of the bad boys, and there were a lot of people scared of him because he was a fighter. He used to do things I hated like going to WT Edwards (a detention center for juveniles) and staying for 21 days at a time. I didn't like the time we spent away from each other. It triggered something in me that I now know was the abandonment syndrome.

He was the first boy to buy me a promise ring. LOL! At that age, what were we promising? He used to tell me that he loved me all the time. Deep down inside, I knew he did, and at that age he didn't know how to choose between what he felt made him happy (being a bad boy) and me. Things were good for our age; I liked him and so did my mom because she remembered him from the old neighborhood. He used to write me letters while he was away. The last letter that he wrote me I kept for years, at least until I was 17 years old. I still have the promise ring. I had never heard a male speak to or about me the way he did. I felt special. But I hated it because all the males in my life, by that point, had told me they loved me, but they always left me.

# Reflection

From a child to my adulthood, I've always stayed in my head. The lies of the enemy were like a song on repeat. I believed everything he said about me, my family, and my future. I was searching for something, and I didn't know what it was. But I now know that I was searching for something to validate me. I couldn't be what I thought because there was something deep within that knew I was something more than what I was currently living.

*Take a moment and think of a time where God kept you and you didn't know it. Recall how God kept you.*

_____

_____

_____

_____

_____

_____

_____

_____

# SEARCHING FOR WHAT'S MISSING

One rainy day, I reflected to a particular time in my life when things were tough for my mom, brothers, and me. My mom and Frank had called it quits for a few years by then. It wasn't a nasty break up, so I don't remember why exactly. I think I was about 10. My mom had a new boyfriend whom she dated for a couple years, and they were going to the next phase. We moved in with him into his one-bedroom apartment for a couple of weeks. This apartment was in the University area of Tampa that we called "Cross Fletcher," but it was known to city officials as "Suitcase City." It was a rough neighborhood. My mom's boyfriend was great. He lit up my mom's world like I had never seen before. I mean there was something different about this relationship. It wasn't like my mom and dad's relationship nor my younger brother's dad (Frank). She seemed so happy with him while things were falling apart for me.

We moved again, but we stayed in the Cross Fletcher area. We moved into Timberlakes Apartments. The boy that I thought I loved was heading down the wrong path—fast. The last time he went to "WT Edwards," the detention center for juveniles, I decided that was enough. I didn't want that behavior in my life. I was hurt because, at the time, that was the only male in my life who understood me and loved me. My dad didn't want me. My relationship with my older brother had taken a turn for the worse. My brother and I fought **ALL** the time. I hated fighting with my brother when he was supposed to love me and protect me. I felt that he hated me like my dad. My mom's new boyfriend, whom I quickly called my stepdad, was now part of my life. I knew he cared for me, but it wasn't the same. Knowing Sedrick from age nine to twelve felt like an eternity.

During that time, my mom and I weren't getting along. I felt like she hated me too. Everything I did landed me in trouble. That was the only attention I was getting. I felt totally ignored. My brothers were always getting in trouble, but I tried not to. I spent a lot of time away from home just to escape the madness of that life.

I started contemplating leaving the earth, I

thought it would be the best thing. I didn't know how to deal with those feelings, so I started saying the Lord's Prayer again. Living in Timberlakes was cool, but it had its pros and cons like everything else. When we moved into those apartments, we met residents that we instantly hit it off with and became friends. It was a small complex, but there were children of all ages that enabled my brothers and I to gain friends. We all hung out in the complex and did not go far because Suitcase City wasn't a place where you wanted to get caught up.

By this time, our three-bedroom apartment was too crowded for me. It was good for a while, but the girl, Laya, who my older brother was dating became pregnant and was no longer allowed to live where she resided. My mother, being who she is, allowed Laya to live with us. I was irritated because, once again, I was forced to share the little attention I received. It was difficult. I set aside my feelings and befriended her. Things were great.

We became good friends; I trusted her. We had a lot of talks about things and spent time together. Some of the conversations made me feel uneasy, but I was a big girl, and I wasn't going to show her that I couldn't handle the conversations. There were conversations that left me with a heightened sense of wonder. Some of our conversations made me feel that I was missing something and that I should have a boyfriend.

Sedrick and I had been broken up for months by then. I wanted a male figure in my life. There was a boy named Nardo who lived in the complex. We connected like siblings instantly. He became my best friend. He was a little older than me, but it was like we could read one another. We talked about things, and I was able to share things with him that I didn't share with anyone, things like my real feelings. There was a green tank or something behind his building that we used to sit on and talk. We mostly sat there when I needed to talk. Oftentimes, no one knew we were there. We would always meet outside before anyone came out. He was like my counselor. There was absolutely no judgment. He was my safe place.

There was a boy named Antoine who also lived in the apartment complex, Antoine was my second boy-friend. He was different than Sedrick. He was a good boy. He was a six feet tall, dark-skinned, slender guy with bowlegs. It was the legs that grabbed my atten-tion. He was a meek and mild young man. Antoine was so easy going, and he had a crush on me. Since

I broke up with Sed, I was feeling empty. I didn't know I could talk to God and He would be there for me. I didn't know how to pray. Instead, I did what I knew how to do and that was fill the void. One night while sitting with my new best friend, Nardo, I spotted this guy.

I said, "**WHO IS THAT?**"

Nardo raised a brow with confusion on his face, "Where?"

I pointed, "Right there with them white jeans on."

He looked at me with a puzzled face and called him by his nickname, "Ducey."

"WHAT?" my voice screeched with excitement.

Although he had a crush on me, I thought he was cute, but not my type. Until that night.

I said, "Nardo, I thought he was in Chicago." By the tone of my voice, he was probably thinking that something was going on in my head.

Nardo turned and looked at me with a smile on his face like I had never seen before in the year that I had known him. He was Antoine's best friend, too.

"Why are are smiling?" I smirked at Nardo.

"Because I see it."

"See what?" I looked at him from the corner of my eye.

He laughed. I smiled.

"Tell him to come over here."

Antoine was standing there under the light pole wearing white jeans and a Charlotte Hornets starter jacket. His shirt, shoes, and hat all matched. I always had a thing for boys who dressed nice because my brother did, and from what I could remember about my dad, so did he. My stepdad was also ALWAYS dressed nice, so I knew that was necessary for a male in my life.

I admired him, from head to toe, as he walked over. He was bowlegged, which made this boy sexy to me. When he got over to where we were, he was smiling and so was I. Then, I noticed the gold teeth in his mouth. I fell head over heels. That night we decided to be boyfriend and girlfriend. I was 12 and a half at the time, so I felt that I was old enough to have a real boyfriend.

Time went on and I continued to say The Lord's Prayer because I felt better, and I didn't feel as lonely. Things were good. I was finally happy as I masked it and I started to believe that I wasn't missing anything, and my life was good. Even though we were young, I could see that Antoine really cared for me. He treated me like a young lady, and he always pursued me. We spent a lot of time together because we lived so close. Living in our neighborhood, we moved in groups because it was the safest way. We all went to the mall together, we would go to the park together, and even walked to "Malibu Grand Prix" together. Some of those times were scary. There were times that we had to run all the way home because of gang activity. God kept us because bullets were flying, and we all made it home safe. There were times when all the teens from the complex were sitting outside on the stairs of a building and without warning, we would be surrounded by the "Green Team" with their guns drawn. Green Team was a special Sheriff's force that was put together for that part of the city. That was another reason why we traveled in groups. I can't count the number of times Green Team jumped out of vans with guns drawn on our crowd of teens. It was sad, but it became our norm. We were scared every time because we didn't know if we were going to make it home. As I think back now, one wrong move could have ended one of our lives. Most of the times they ran our names in the system. While they were running our names, we were held at gun point. I didn't tell my mom how often it happened because I didn't want to have to stay home while everyone went out, especially Antoine. We learned to tread lightly.

Antoine and I made the best of our relationship. His sister and I were friends, and his mother liked me for the little girl I was. I loved him and I had his name plastered all over my walls. I had things like the handwritten pictures that said, "Shay loves Antoine," "Antoine (heart) Shay," "S and A forever," or just his name in assorted colors. However, things between us were not always easy. We would have little arguments and be upset with one another. His mom would have talks with us. LOL! It's funny now as I think back, how cute! Even though we argued, we continued our relationship.

I turned 13. We were about 10 months into the relationship, which was forever for us. One day my mom and stepdad went out. They left Laya and I at home, and we had some friends come by. We were all listening to music and dancing, having a good time. I danced until I was sick; so, I went into the house and got into my bed. My heart was beating extremely fast. I thought I was going to vomit, and my head was pounding. After a few moments, my heart rate slowed, my head stopped hurting, and I didn't feel sick anymore. I laid there a little while longer to gather myself. My door opened, I thought it was my mom, but it was Antoine.

"Are you okay?" Antoine questioned.

"I think so." I looked at him.

He sat next to me and began to gently rub my back for a second.

Antione looked at me as his forehead creased with concern. "I just was checking on you."

He stayed and we were laughing and talking like always. The lights were not on in the room, but we could still see each other. There was a light pole right outside my window and it was able to light up the room a little. The door opened again, and that's when things changed. It was Laya.

"What y'all doing?" Laya had a smirk on her face.

We said, in unison, "Nothing."

She smirked and chuckled, "Oh, I thought y'all was hunching."

Since I was still a virgin I said, "NO!"

She grinned, "I would be."

He frowned, "She's not ready for that."

She closed the door and walked away. There was dead silence in the room.

Then I asked him, "How do you know that I'm not ready?"

At that moment, all the sex conversations Laya and I been having, came to mind. I mean most of my friends were having sex. I thought that I should try it, too.

I looked at him; he was staring at the wall. "I'm ready."

He turned and looked back at me. "Are you sure?"

My nerves were on end. "Yeah."

"Okay, I will be right back."

I raised up quickly from my lying position. "Where are you going?"

"I need to go get protection."

I was 13. He was 15.

My eyes popped out of my head, "Wait! If you leave, everyone will know."

"I will go out the back so no one will see me." He was referring to all our friends because they were all still outside listening to music and dancing.

He did as he said and when he came back, I felt scared. He looked at me and I believe he saw my fear.

He asked one more time, "Are you sure?"

"Yes!" My voice quivered.

I started to think of all the stories I had heard about girls losing their virginity and how horrible it was. My story was different. He was gentle. He kept asking if I was okay or if he was hurting me during the process, and as quickly as it started, it was over. I thought, *That's it*! It was not a horrifying experience, but it was a quick one. Afterwards, he asked me again if I was okay because he knew that it was my first time.

I said, "Yeah, I think so."

He went to the restroom and came back. When I went to the restroom to clean up, there was blood. *Was that supposed to happen?* I was scared that something was wrong. But as scared as I was, I wasn't going to show him. I came back and sat on the side of the bed next to him and I couldn't believe what just happened. I held my head down in disbelief because I knew I wasn't ready, but I wanted to be a part of the group of girls that could say I lost my virginity. It was supposed to make me feel grown, right? We sat there in silence for a minute, and he hugged me, but we didn't talk.

After a couple of minutes or so, I said, "Let's go outside with everyone."

I wanted to go outside to forget what had happened. Not in a bad way because the experience wasn't horrific, but I wasn't ready. I just wanted to have something to talk about with Laya and the other girls. I was told already several times that I should do it. It seemed like all the boys wanted the girls that were having sex. I felt bad about it, but later came to understand the reason—**early conviction**. I just wanted to fit in. We joined the others outside and everyone was inquiring. "What were you all doing?" They made kissy faces. I didn't say a word.

"Nothing, chilling waiting for her to feel better." Antoine remained calm.

I just looked at him. I will never forget one of our friends looked at him and said, "That was fast. All this happened in like a 30 to 40-minute time span."

His facial expression remained the same, "Yeah, she was tired. What are you talking about?"

The friend said, "Yeah, okay."

I felt like he knew something. I was wondering if I had some indicator on me because I was looking at Antoine and he looked completely normal, so it had to be me. I was afraid that when my momma got home, she was going to know, too, because it had to be on me somewhere, so I made sure I showered good. But when they returned home, we were already in bed asleep. The next morning, I woke up early and took another shower to be sure I was clean, with no evidence. We lived on the bottom floor in the complex, so I went outside with my bowl of cereal and sat on the stairs. I didn't want to be in the house when anyone woke up. As I sat there, I noticed I was a little sore in my vaginal area. I continued sitting on the stairs just looking at the world around me. I walked to the dumpster to pour out the milk from my cereal and went back to sit on the stairs. A minute later, I looked to the left and saw Antoine walking toward me. "Hey."

"Hey," I responded back.

He asked, "Are you okay?"

"Yes." He sat next to me, and we didn't talk for a while, but it seemed that our connection was deeper. We just sat there, and I was thinking, *"Okay, this is the part where he breaks up with me."* After a couple of minutes, he didn't say he wanted to break up, so I felt relieved because, from the stories I heard, I thought after that night things were going to be over between us. I didn't know then that a soul tie had formed. A soul tie is when you connect with someone, not always sexually, but intimately, and you let them into your soul and where parts of their spirit are imparted in you and yours in them.

We continued to date and before long it was summer again. He had a summer job; the year was

1994. I was going to be 14 and I still had the same boyfriend. I felt that I had beat the odds because, according to all the stories, we were supposed to have broken up by now. Every morning of that summer I would get up when my mom left for work and go to his house. I went to wake him up for work. I sat and watched TV until he was ready. Once he was ready, we would leave his house and I would walk him halfway to work. He worked at the park by our house. I was cool with walking with him because it only took a few minutes. I would go back home and feel some type of way. It seemed like he was leaving me for good every day when he kissed me goodbye. It seemed like that kiss was something that held his love until the next time I saw him. I realized that I had an issue with goodbyes. They seemed so permanent.

I knew what time he got off work, so I would walk to meet him halfway. He was as happy to see me as I was to see him; he would greet me with a hug. I was in what I knew, and thought, was love. His mom had a guy friend that she was seeing, and he was the nicest. He would always talk with us. He used to always tease us about being together. He would tell us that we were in love. I knew that it felt right.

After turning 14 and starting junior high school,

ninth grade, there were a lot of boys interested in me. I got a lot of attention. Antoine was now in high school, and he was getting the same attention with him being a dark chocolate, bow-legged dude that dressed nice and smelled good all the time. Our lives started to drift apart. We tried to hold it together, but it just didn't work. That was hard on our relationship and things were hard at home. My mom was doing her best with what she had, but sometimes things were too much. Even though she tried to hold it together, my older brother and I saw the struggle. The $165 bi-weekly child support wasn't enough either. I didn't know how to deal with issues in the house and issues in a relationship.

One day Antoine and I got into this huge argument because I **thought** that he was being unfaithful to me. I used that to my advantage. This was a way for me to escape what felt good. My emotions were all over the place. I didn't know how to appreciate happiness. I was so used to the feeling of abandonment and rejection that I started to create it for myself.

I said, "I want to break up."

He said, "Okay."

He didn't really want to break up, but because I did, he went along with it.

As much as it hurt, I thought that it was the right thing to do because I was going to get out before I got hurt. I felt that I was getting too close to him, and I didn't want to. The two examples of relationships I saw with my mom left her sad and broken - our dad and my younger brother's dad. I didn't want that. Those were my examples. Although I never saw that with my current stepdad, I waited for it to happen.

There was a guy, Tweety, a mutual friend of ours that I knew was really into me, but I didn't entertain him before because I was head over heels with Antoine. But that day I was so mad that I told Nardo to let Tweety know that I wanted to talk to him, and he did. Tweety was light skinned with slight bowlegs. He stood about five feet ten inches, and he was my bad boy from Miami. I heard many times that I slowed him down. Tweety was truly a thug. He was everything I thought a bad boy was and I liked it. There were plenty of times that he scared me with some of the things he did and told me about. One thing about him was I always felt protected. Not only was he my boyfriend, he became my best friend. Tweety came into the apartments, and I stood and spoke to him right in front of Antoine. Antoine was furious. They played little league football together and I was a cheerleader for their team, so we were all at practice together. I had my cheerleading friends, and we were all close.

So, to get back at me, Antoine approached one of my friends and made her his girlfriend. I was also **FURIOUS**! So, Kevin, his mom's guy friend sat us both down and talked to us. He told me that I had hurt Antoine. I didn't believe him, but when I looked at Antoine, he had a tear in his eye. I remembered not caring because I was mad about him making my friend his girlfriend. As time went on, Antoine and I redeveloped our friendship. One day we had sex and considered getting back together, but I didn't want to because I liked the guy I was talking to. But Antoine and the girl broke up. He started having many girlfriends. Tweety started coming around every day. We started spending a lot of time together. We went to school together, rode the same bus, and sat together. He would carry my books, we would dress alike, and he always gave me money. I never questioned where he got the money. I just knew that he shared. There were so many girls in love with him. He was a hot topic, immensely popular, and there I was with him as my boyfriend. The girl that couldn't keep it together. The girl with many insecurities that were buried behind a smile and an outgoing personality. The things I went through in my family I kept to myself. I wasn't sharing with Nardo as much anymore, but we were still close. I just didn't want to let him into the new places of struggle.

Girls in the school wanted to fight me about Tweety. I couldn't believe it. He would argue with the girls for talking about me. He always threatened to jump in the fight if they ever tried to fight me. I felt so protected. Early in our relationship, he told me that he really liked me and that he thought he loved me. For me that was music to my ears. A male to tell me that he loved me again. Antoine was the last to tell me that, so once we broke up, I didn't hear it and that void started to open again. But once Tweety started saying it, it was what I thought I needed at 14 and a half years old.

At home, things were getting tough again, it was like we fell into a rough patch. There was a period that we didn't have a car. But that didn't stop my mom from going to work and getting us to school. She had such a determination to make a better life for us. There was a morning that I would never forget. My mom got us up, we started to get dressed. She made sure that we were all bundled up because it was cold that morning. We had to catch two public transportation buses to get to our destination. We caught the first bus, then had to sit at the stop waiting for our next bus. We were freezing! I looked at my mom and I could tell that she was sad. There were no tears, but I saw it in her face as she looked at us with disappointment. She was disappointed in herself, and I could see it. We were all shivering and bunched together. My mom said, "We are going home. It's too cold out here. We will try it again tomorrow." In a couple of weeks, we had a car.

Living this impoverished lifestyle taught me some tough life lessons. It also gave me a "strive harder" attitude about life. I watched my mom never give up. Even with tears in her eyes she kept pushing to make sure that she provided for us to the best of her abilities. My stepdad did his part, but I watched my mom push through all the hard times.

I always looked for things to bury myself in, junk food, juices, and sodas, never water. Because of that, I had recurring bladder infections. They were so bad at times that walking hurt. One day I stayed home from school because I was in pain, so Tweety stayed home too. Later that day he came over. Laya and I were home alone. He came into my room, and as I laid on my stomach, he laid his head on my back and we watched TV.

"What y'all doing?" Laya asked, walking into the room. We told her nothing. It felt like Déjà vu. She gave me that look again and said, "That might help your stomach."

I had just taken medicine, so I was feeling fine. I knew what she meant, and I wanted to have sex with him, but I wasn't going to. Still, I thought more about it. **IT** started to happen. We were a few minutes in when my door opened. I thought it was Laya again, but much to my surprise, it was my uncle. I thought that I was going to die. This was the same uncle who made me his dance partner when I was younger. He had moved in with us.

He looked and said, "Put your clothes on."

We did and sat there for a minute. Anyone that knew my uncle knew that **he didn't play**. He said what he meant and meant what he said. So now we were both thinking that we were going to die. I started crying, like boohooing. So, a couple of minutes later my uncle came back into the room. We were nervous as EVER! He started to talk, and as he was speaking, I saw Tweety looking around the room. My uncle talked and talked. I didn't hear much of what he said after he told me that I had to tell my mom. Now I was thinking I was going to die twice. He told Tweety, "Let me talk to you outside while she calls her mom." It was at that instant I realized he meant business as he left my room. I was thinking how I was going to tell Tweety's mom that my uncle killed him for having sex with me. I was all kinds of messed up. Why wasn't the door locked? Because you didn't lock doors in my momma's house.

So, when my uncle stepped out and went to wait for Tweety on the stairs, I asked him, "Why were you looking around my room?"

He said, "You know your uncle is crazy. I was looking for something to hit him so I could get away if he tried to kill me."

When they went outside, Laya came running in my room where I was crying because I thought this was my last day on earth.

She said, "I'm so sorry. I didn't hear him come up. I would have warned you."

I didn't believe her then and I still don't believe it to this day. I called my mom, and we had a conversation; then, she asked me if I was having sex and I told her, "Yes." She hung the phone up in my face. I was scared. I started packing because I knew I was going to **die** or be put out. Neither one of those things happened, as I am here to tell the story.

Living in Suitcase City had started to take a toll on my older brother and me. The peer pressure there was ridiculous. I can say when the enemy started in on us, he was on us. I recalled coming home and finding out that my brother had a gun and shot out the back-sliding glass door. He was 16. I don't know where, how, or why he had a gun, but weird and crazy things were happening. It was time for us to move. I told some of my friends in the complex that we were moving. I didn't tell Antoine; his sister did. I saw Antoine every day and he still had a piece of my heart. After the dust settled, we were friends again. I was sad when it was time to leave him because I thought one day we would try again. Although I loved Tweety, there was still something that I loved and respected about Antoine. It was my first soul tie.

It looked to me like the males that were in my life were leaving. Although I was the one moving, leaving Antoine felt like he was leaving me. Tweety transferred to another school. Being in school without him was lonely for a week or two. When we moved to East Tampa on a street called "New Orleans," the move caused me to switch schools, and I ended up at

Van Buren Junior High, the same school that Tweety attended. I was excited to see him at school every day. When I got to the school there were people there that I knew. I wasn't nervous at all, but all the people I didn't know there knew me. When I got there, people were like, "Oh, you're Shay!"

And we were back at it again. Having lunch together, him walking me to my classes, waiting for me after school to walk me to the bus, and writing letters. I received a letter every other day from him expressing his love. It was the teenage dating life. I felt loved and protected. The seed of rejection was losing life. He saw me! He saw me for who I was, there was no need to mask. He loved me and all my broken pieces. He was careful with me, somehow, he understood that I was fragile. As tough as I was, he allowed me to be delicate and never made me feel less than on my weak days or the days I couldn't figure out my feelings, when my emotions were all over the place. I thought that we were perfect together. I finally had a male in my life that I got it right with.

I finished my ninth-grade year and started to enjoy the summer with him. We were together all the time, sometimes from sunup to sundown. Summer was good when we moved into our new house and away from Cross Fletcher. We moved across the street from one of my mom's close friend's sister. She had children who I got to know. She had a daughter the same age as me and one younger than me. That was cool. Fall came and things started to change. Prayer had become distant for me again. I wasn't praying, and everything was good, so I thought that I was okay.

It was time to return to school, and Tweety and I were no longer attending the same school. I started at Hillsborough High School. He went to Chamberlain High School; however, by the second week of school, he was at Hillsborough, too. It was the first day of school and I was there alone, no Tweety. As I walked into this huge building, I thought to myself, *what in the world!* I received my schedule, and I went to my first class. A little nerve-racking, but okay. That class was in a portable; I thought I was going to get lost in that school. The bell rang and it was time to change classes. I walked down the hallway and I heard someone say, "Vallerie!" I didn't know if it was her, but that was a name I hadn't heard since the fifth grade. I turned and there she stood as she talked to whoever called her name. I smiled with the biggest smile. She was about to walk away.

I said, "Vallerie!"

She turned and paused. Once she spotted me, we ran to one another and hugged. Our next class was together. We walked and talked, and things didn't seem so frightening. It was time to go to Homeroom. I found a seat toward the back and sat there thinking about my boyfriend, when I heard a male voice say, "Shay!" I looked up and it was one of my classmates from junior high school. After the bell rang, everyone settled down. The teacher started to call names. After a couple of names, the teacher said, "Aislyn Coney." I looked up because that was a name I hadn't heard since my time in the Head Start program. That was my friend's name back then, and I always wondered about her. It was her; I wondered if she remembered me. She did. That was amazing. At that point, I believed that Hillsborough was going to be something awesome.

The day went on, class after class, and I saw more people that I knew. It was weird how there was a blend from first-year students to seniors. I went home excited to tell my mom all about it.

By the time Tweety got to Hillsborough, I was comfortable. But things were back to normal with him there. A month or so passed and he started missing days of school. He left Hillsborough and went to "Hillsborough Adult." Hillsborough Adult was a school that you attended to get your GED if you dropped out and wanted to get your high school diploma. This school was across the street, so when I got out, he would meet me at the corner, and we would walk home together with my friends. Because we were at different schools and he wasn't there often, things between us started to change. There were boys, boys, and more boys, so getting a lot of attention didn't allow me to miss him too much. I was having so much fun at school, I wanted to be there every day. There were so many cute boys I found myself interested in, but I wouldn't make friends with any one of them because I was only a tenth grader, and I had a boyfriend. I attended my first high school football game and thought, *Man, this is amazing.*

By September, things with Tweety and I were shaky and ending. We started to argue a lot and broke up. I made male and female friends. The year was 1995-96 and high school was all I thought it was going to be. Tweety and I were done.

I was sitting in Math class, and I was talking to one of my friends, Victoria. The teacher was calling students to the front of the classroom to get their assigned book from him. I was sitting talking because that's what I was good at. The teacher called a name, and I didn't budge or look to see who he was calling. I wasn't interested because it wasn't my name.

Then this tall, fine young man walked past me. I immediately stopped talking and started to look at him as he walked to the front of the classroom. I checked him out starting from his butt since it was eye level while I was sitting. My eyes slowly strolled down to his legs. He had the sexiest bowlegs to me. I watched his legs as he walked to get his book and, when he turned around to go back to his seat, I gazed at him from head to toe. I admired his physique as it reminded me of an athlete. I still remember what he was wearing. He had on a white t-shirt, white jean shorts, with white socks and white shoes. He was handsome with his caramel brown skin. As he was walking back to his seat, he saw me looking at him. We locked eyes and my heart skipped a beat. We looked at each other until he passed me. He had gentle eyes. I leaned over to Victoria, smiled, and said, "I'm gonna get him. That's going to be my boyfriend."

She looked at me and we laughed. After class, I was on a search to find out information about him. I was on a mission. I had a friend named Charles who knew everyone. I saw Charles and got right in his face.

"Charles, WHO IS THAT?" I asked.

Charles chuckled. "Who, Elijah?"

"Who?" I sounded like an owl.

"Elijah. We call him E."

I grinned from ear to ear. "YES!"

"Oh, you like him?" Charles looked at me with his lips slightly turned up on both ends.

I nodded yes, with the same big smile.

I almost choked when Charles said, "I will tell him."

"No! Find out if he has a girlfriend."

"Okay." Charles walked away, and I silently prayed Elijah didn't have a girlfriend.

A few days later, Charles got back to me. "I don't think he has a girlfriend, and he plays football and basketball."

I thought, *oh really,* as I tapped my chin with my index finger. I started to watch him for a couple of days, and I noticed that he was incredibly quiet. I had never really seen him talking to many people. I forget how I got his phone number, but I got it! I called him and we talked for a little while. I told him that I thought he was cute and that I liked him. A few weeks passed and we talked a few more times on the phone, then we started speaking in school. I was making progress. One day he said that he was going to come over after practice. He went home, showered, and called.

He said, "Hey, I'm going to come over."

I jumped in the shower. I wanted to be smelling good when he arrived. I lotion myself down with one of my favorite scents, "Pear Glace," by Victoria's Secret. He came over and we sat on my porch and talked. Every day after that he would go home, shower, and come to my house. **EVERY DAY**. That was a big deal back then. Guys courted girls; they pursued them. Sometimes Charles would come as well because Vallerie used to be over at my house, too. Our front porch was a hangout for me and some of my closest friends. My mom had her own home daycare, so she was home all the time. This was important to me because she was able to meet my friends and guide me as needed. My relationship with my mom was a lot better than before as we developed an open relationship. Things were good at home; we were finally stable.

****

## I HATE GIRL DRAMA!

One day I found out that my friend across the street was also interested in Elijah. We were all sitting on the porch, about seven or eight of us. We were listening to music and having an enjoyable time. I went into the house for something.

She (my friend) then went to Elijah and asked, "Can I talk to you for a minute?"

Elijah, being the guy that he was, replied, "Yes."

When I returned to the porch, I looked around confused and noticed that Elijah and my friend were missing.

Vallerie said to me, "She asked Elijah can she talk to him for a minute."

I said, "Oh!" with a puzzled face, but I didn't think anything of it.

I saw them walking back from down the street. My friend who was normally perky no longer seemed like herself. To me, she was upset because she didn't return to the porch. Instead, she went to her house across the street.

Elijah walked up to the gate and asked to talk to me. I was confused as to what happened. We walked down the street so that we could talk privately.

"Do you know what she wanted?" Elijah asked me.

"No." I was totally confused.

"She demanded me to choose between her and you, "Elijah responded, appearing as confused as I was.

I looked up at him, as he stood six-foot two, towering over me and I said, "What did you choose?"

He responded, "Where am I standing and who am I talking to?"

I melted. There was this warm feeling that filled my body from head to toe. I gazed into his brown eyes, and I smiled, and he did, too. That was the point I knew that we were a thing. We started talking more in school and he continued to come over, every day, after practice. We enjoyed each other's company. I supported him the only way I knew how, at the time. I went to his games and watched him play. I made sure that people knew I was his #1 fan even though he had many.

He was a great ball player; I would tell him how well he did just to see his smile. There were times that I would visit him, and the phone would ring with college scouts wanting to talk to him or speak with his dad. Being the gentle giant that he was he never allowed the spotlight to interfere with his humbleness. I mean, college scout after college scout used to call his house. I was amazed. By looking at him and talking with him, you would have never known all of that was happening. That was the first time I saw what being humble looked like. We dated for a while, the average high school dating length. The funny thing was, he never told me that he loved me, but his actions showed it and I admit now that I didn't know how to read the cues. Cues like riding his bike to my house until he got a car. Opening doors, complimenting me, he gave me eye contact while listening attentively, letting me lean on him when I needed a safe place, making me a priority in his life. Neither one of us had much, but we gave what we could and most of it was time to one another. That type of love I wasn't used to. It didn't look like the love that I had become accustomed to. I didn't know that then, but that is what love should have looked like all my life.

He was loving, kind, compassionate, and understanding. He listened with his heart and when he responded, he used his words carefully. Our conversations were incomparable to any other that I had thus far. We had a connection that ran deep, and as great as he was, I didn't think that I was the girl for him. I believed the lies of the devil. I was working through some stuff within myself like self-esteem issues. There was still a complexion complex that I couldn't overcome. As much as I masked it, I still believed deep down that I was too black and ugly.

Because of his intellect, I felt that he would figure me out because I was so comfortable talking to him. I thought there was a chance that he would slip pass my guard and I didn't want to let anyone into that place. That guarded place had become my norm and that was okay. I couldn't allow him to shake up things now, because my fake confidence was working for me. I call it fake because I suppressed everything that gave me a feeling that I didn't know or like. I wanted to take him seriously, but I couldn't. I was afraid he would take me to the highest peak of happiness and let me fall without catching me or without me knowing how to fly. Insecurity, rejection, abandonment, and my trust issues wouldn't allow me to fully enjoy the pleasure he brought into my life. I told myself on countless occasions that he wasn't that into me, so I wasn't going to let him into my heart. To keep from falling in love with Elijah, I found someone to distract me and my heart.

There was this guy named Kevin. You see Kevin reminded me of my dad in a lot of ways. I know that was a part of my attraction to him. He wasn't tall, he stood five feet nine inches, two inches taller than me. He was a well-dressed chocolate man with the smoothest dark skin I had ever seen. There was something about his cocoa brown colored eyes that hypnotized me. He was always well-groomed. His silky jet-black hair made me seasick, he had so many waves. I found him very attractive, but he had a girlfriend. I didn't care, I just wanted to be his friend. I watched him whenever I saw him around the school or walking home from school. I believe he knew there was an attraction, so he would walk down my street on purpose.

May 29, 1996, it was "Senior Send-Off," and I knew if I was going to talk to him that it had to be that day. I sat in class and wrote this long letter telling him how I thought he was cute. I told him that I was aware that he had a girlfriend. I also had a boyfriend. I wanted him to know before he left that I was interested in getting to know him. I gave him my number and told him to call me. Days went by and I didn't hear from him; it was cool. However, I felt some kind of way. On June 6th, I was laying in my mother's bed and the phone rang.

I answered, "Hello!"

There was this deep Barry White baritone voice on the other end of the phone that said, "May I speak to Shay?"

At that moment, my heart started to race.

"This is she, who is this?" I replied.

"This Kevin."

I sat up and smiled ear-to-ear as I responded, "What's up?"

The conversation was short. He was getting ready for graduation, and they had to be there early. We talked about a few things, nothing memorable. Then, he asked if I was coming to graduation. I told him that I would see him there.

Right after we hung up, I called Vallerie excited! "Girl, guess who just called me?"

"Who?" she asked.

"The dude!"

"Which dude?" she questioned.

"Kevin!" It took everything in me not to scream.

"Oh, for real!" she sounded surprised.

"Yes!" I hollered into the phone like only a teenage girl would.

She laughed through her words, "You ready to go to graduation now, right?"

"Heck yeah!" I wanted to jump out of my skin with excitement.

On that day, Kevin and I became friends and there was something about him that I was really attracted to. It was summer. Elijah and I were drifting apart, and Tweety and I were back to hanging out, not as much as the summer before, but we were trying to keep it together as friends.

One day, Tweety and his friend Keith came to my house. They were in this nice Mercedes Benz. I asked whose car they were in, and Keith said, "My uncle's." I left with them, and we rode around all day, just riding with no real purpose other than to be seen in a nice car.

I knew Tweety started selling drugs after we broke up, so we didn't spend much time together. We just remained friends. I didn't care about him selling drugs because I got whatever I wanted from him. It was a terrible mentality to have, but I was a teenager that didn't know better at the time. While we were hanging out, there was something that didn't feel right about the car we were in. I ignored it. I trusted Tweety and I knew Keith, so I believed they wouldn't put me in harm's way. While we rode around, I held down the passenger seat. No backseat for me. It started to get dark.

They said, "Let's take you home."

I was good with that because we had spent the entire day together. We turned off a side street on to Fletcher Avenue, and there was a car riding behind us. We didn't pay it any attention because there was nothing that stood out about the car. We pulled up to the stop light on the corner of Fletcher and Nebraska Avenue. The next thing I remember, there were police EVERYWHERE! Guns pulled and pointed at us. My heart dropped because I had no idea what was going on. The officer swung the door open, threw me to the ground, and cuffed me. My pager fell out, and his knee was in my back.

I was petrified as I uttered, "My beeper, my beeper, it fell out!"

The officer picked me up with the cuffs on. He looked at me, and by the look on his face I knew he could tell that I was terrified. He called a female cop over to search me, and she did. As she frisked me, I felt that all my private space was violated, as I had never been touched in those places by a woman or without permission. The more she touched me the more violated I felt. I wanted it all to be over in that moment.

After searching me, she stated, "She's clean."

He looked at me, still seeing fright on my face. "Do you know what's going on?" he asked.

With tears in my eyes I said, "No!" I closed my eyes for a brief second and the tears streamed down my face.

The captain came over.

He said to the cop that slammed me to the ground, "She looks terrified."

The cop said, "I don't think she knows what's going on."

I looked around and saw Keith in one cop car and Tweety in another.

I was still standing in the middle of Fletcher Avenue talking to the cops. There were people looking on, and I was nervous that someone would recognize me and call my mom or brother.

"Sir, I don't know why this is happening." I held back my tears.

The captain looked at me with an understanding face, calmly stating, "You were in a stolen car."

I almost fainted. He grabbed me, looked to the officer who cuffed me, and said, "Take the cuffs off of her."

He called the female cop over and as she walked towards me, I thought I was going to jail, too. Instead, he said, "Take this baby home."

That was my first and last time being handcuffed and in the back of a police car. On the ride home, all I was thinking was *should I go home? My momma gon' kill me. Maybe I should go somewhere else for the night.* The officer was talking to me all the way home. I didn't hear one word she said. I was wondering what was going to happen when my mom found out.

When I got home that night it was about eleven o'clock. I opened the door, and my mom was sitting there on the couch with a look of disappointment all over her face. I didn't get a chance to explain because Tweety had already called her from a pay phone. Although she looked at me with disappointment, she was more concerned with me being okay. Once she saw that I was fine, she went to bed without a word. Things between Tweety and I changed. I was angry at myself for trusting him and angry at him for putting me in that position.

I was still talking to Elijah, but not as much because that summer he went away to basketball camp. While he was gone, I filled my time with friends. The distance caused us to drift apart. When he returned, I spent time with him while he was recovering from an injury he endured while at camp. Although we weren't a couple anymore, we were still friends and I cared about his well-being. School was back on, and it was my junior year. The distance between Tweety and I was inevitable, so by September we decided to no longer be friends. I was hurt.

I didn't want him to be a part of my life anymore. I knew that he loved me, but the streets were calling him, and he wanted to go.

He expressed himself to me saying, "I love you, Shay! I really do, but I feel me going in another direction and I don't want to take you with me. You a good girl and I know that, so this is why we have to end this."

I believed him. He told me all about the girl he was dating and how she gave him money to flip and make more money selling drugs. I didn't want it to end, but I respected the decision. We sat on the curb, he gave me one last hug and left. I went in the house and cried. Not only was I losing a boy that I thought would love me forever, but I was losing a good friend. From childhood, it felt like I was always losing the men who were important to me.

****

It was October… Homecoming time, and I needed a date. No one at school had asked me, not even Elijah. So, I asked Tweety. We still talked periodically, so he agreed. Now that I had a date, I couldn't wait to dress up and feel like a princess. It was my first dance since the seventh grade.

The excitement was high! I spent days looking for

the perfect colors and a dress that we could afford. Finding the right shoes so that I was able to dance, but be comfortable at the same time, that was key. Looking through hair magazines to find the perfect hairstyle. I wanted to rent the perfect car. I had my driver's license, and I was driving to Homecoming. Yes, honey! No drop offs for me! From what I recall, October 16, 1996 was Homecoming day. I get goosebumps thinking back on it.

I went to the salon early that morning to get my hair done. I was too excited when I left the salon to meet my "bestie," Vallerie, at the nail shop. All Homecoming tasks complete? Check! I was ready. I picked up Tweety; he got dressed in the back room of my house. We were both dressed around the same time, and we walked out of our dressing areas at the same time, not knowing the other was dressed. In the four years Tweety had been in my life, I had never seen him in a suit. I must say he looked snazzy. It felt like we took hundreds of pictures the number of times I heard the camera click. Then the time had come; it was time to go. I was nervous and excited at the same time. It felt like butterflies got loose in my stomach. I was nervous because I didn't know whether Elijah was going to be there or if Kevin would be there with his girlfriend. Either way, I was planning to have a wonderful time.

We went to Homecoming and lit up the dance floor from the time we walked in. We ate and laughed, like we didn't have a care in the world. I was grateful neither Elijah nor Kevin was there. After Homecoming, Tweety called a friend to pick him up. I was fine with him leaving because my friends wanted to go out to eat so we could spend more time out. There were at least twenty of us from Homecoming at the restaurant. Of course, Elijah was there with a few of his friends, so I was glad Tweety didn't come. I would have balled up somewhere hoping for miraculous invisibility. When I got to the restaurant, I was wearing Tweety's tuxedo coat because it was cold outside. Elijah didn't talk to me, nor did he make eye contact with me the entire time we were at the restaurant. So, I knew he was NOT happy with me. (Twenty years later, I found out it was because I was wearing Tweety's coat). While eating, everyone was talking about going to an after party. I was going to the after party, too, because I was a part of the "in" crowd. As we were leaving, Elijah walked past me and demanded, "You better go home."

I looked at him and said, "What?"

With a very serious face he said, "You heard what I said."

Because I knew he was serious, I listened, and I went home. I never questioned his reasoning because I already knew why he demanded me to go home instead of the after party. There was going to be under-age drinking, marijuana smoking, and other things that I don't care to mention. Even though he wasn't happy with me, he was still concerned about my safety. I returned home to an empty house. No one was home. It was late, and I was a little afraid. I called Elijah. I explained to him that I was home alone and afraid. This was the biggest house we had lived in by that point, so I wasn't used to so much space. He, and his friends came over and they stayed with me for a while. They left because it was getting late. I went to sleep to keep myself from being scared.

I woke up to my parents coming in. "Where were you?" I asked them.

My mom told me that a close friend of the family had been in a head-on collision, and they were at the hospital. I sat up in my bed looking through my sleepy eyes at her face to see if there had been tears. I was waiting for her to tell me that he died, but she told me that he survived and that he was going to be okay. To this day, no one knew how he escaped death and survived that accident.

She continued by saying, "The doctor said that he was a lucky man."

I was sad because he had a daughter the same age as me. She was an only child, and I couldn't imagine what she was going through knowing that her dad had been in a serious car accident, and he could have lost his life.

Time passed and days went on and things were back to normal from the Homecoming high. We were moving into December. My relationship with Elijah completely faded away. We didn't bring it to a close; we just stopped talking. I began to wonder if I would ever keep a relationship with a man.

Tweety's birthday was in December. That year was his 18th birthday. He came over and we talked. He asked me to hang out with him for his birthday and, of course, I said, "Sure!" I knew I shouldn't hang out with him, but I still cared for him. I thought it would be fun. That night my choices changed my life and took an unexpected turn. It was December 22, 1996. Tweety and I hung out all day. As our day ended, he asked if he could have sex with me one last time. Against all my better judgment, I said, "Yes."

What was the worst that could happen? He was 18 and was of age to get a hotel room. I was 16, and I knew I didn't have any business at a hotel with him. We got there about ten o'clock in the evening. I knew it was getting late and I needed to be home soon. We talked about how much his life had changed in such a brief time and how he still loved me but the road he was heading down clearly wasn't a road for me. So, we had sex and afterwards, he held me and told me he loved me. I fell asleep. I woke up to the vibration of my pager. It was like two o'clock in the morning. I jumped up and saw that it was my mom. *Now I know she is going to kill us!* I hurried and called her.

Calmly she asked, "Where are you? Do you know what time it is? You need to get home now."

I woke him up and said, "I have to go. My mom just paged me." As he checked his pager, he had many missed pages from his girlfriend. We hurried and left the hotel. When I got home, I sat in the car and looked at him. I wanted to cry because I would miss him, but I knew our lives were traveling in different directions. I got out of the car without looking back because I knew that was going to be our last time together.

I got accustomed to my new normal—no boy-friend, no commitment, only male *friends*. Kevin and

I started talking more and getting acquainted. Nothing serious. During that time, I met a guy named Mike. Mike was a very confident young man. I hadn't experienced his type of swag before. He had a decent job and a nice car with stereos that blasted loud music. I loved music, so that was a brownie point for him. He was a dark-skinned brother who stood about five feet eleven inches. Have you heard the saying, "I look a lot different outside of my work clothes"? Well, that was Mike; he was well dressed and always smelled wonderful with the latest cologne. Mike was a good boy with a thug edge. I liked that about him. There were a lot of things I liked about Mike, but my favorite thing was we were both Virgos (and I'm not into astrology), but because of the similarities we shared, I felt we understood each other on a deeper level.

My relationship with Mike had an interesting start. One day we were hanging outside of our houses. Our street was THE STREET. It was where a lot of people hung out. We played four square, two square, jumped rope, raced, you name it. My friend across the street had a boyfriend who would come over often. One day he was over, and he paged his cousin.

The phone rang.

I answered the phone. A pleasant voice on the other side of the phone asked, "Did someone page Mike?"

"Had anyone paged a Mike?" His voice intrigued me, it was a smooth baritone voice. I was curious to see what he looked like. Because if he looked anything like he sounded I wanted to meet him. I was a sucker for deep voices.

Her boyfriend said, "I did."

I gave him the phone. Curiosity was written all over my face, I'm sure. When he hung up the phone, I asked, "Who was that?"

"My cousin."

I smiled.

"What, you like him?"

"No, but he has a sexy voice." My smile grew wide.

He smiled back. "He's on his way over here."

It was another Florida December. It wasn't cold, so we were still able to hang out after dark. Suddenly, we heard loud music blocks over. Her boyfriend said, "That's my cousin. That's Mike!"

*Dang, this dude has a car.* We were standing in anticipation of his arrival as the music got closer and closer. He pulled up with the music pumping loud through his car. He got out. Sexy voice (check), dressed nice (check), and had a car (check, check). I was interested, but I was not going to say anything. Instead, I checked him out. We were all hanging outside when my pager went off. I checked it. It was Kevin. I smiled as I was about to go return his call. Mike, with his sexy self said, "Who is that, your boyfriend? You can tell him not to page you anymore."

I smiled. "Whatever!"

I went in the house to call Kevin. We talked for a few minutes. When I returned outside, I asked Mike, "What did you say?"

"You heard me. Did you tell him not to page you anymore?"

"No. Why would I do that?" I crossed my arms, tilted my head slightly to the side, and stared at him.

With a smirk on his face, filled with cockiness, he leaned against the hood of his car with his arms folded in front of him and said, "Because, you are my girl now."

I laughed and didn't take him seriously, but he was serious. I had already checked him out, and he met all my criteria, so I was okay with that. Kevin was standing me up all the time anyway. He left me wondering most times. I was always his last resort, and I was getting tired of it. Mike came along at the right time. We hit it off, and things with us quickly took off. He went to Brandon High School. He had a job, and it wasn't as a dope boy. I was glad.

Things with us were good. He would leave his school early enough to get me from my school some days. It depended on what time he had to be to work. He would park across the street with his music blasting, of course, and everyone wanted to know who he was. He would stand outside of the car and wait for me. I saw how the girls watched him and made themselves seen. But he was mine, so I didn't worry about them. My friend who stayed across the street rode with us sometimes, but he quickly put that to an end. He would take me for something to eat, then take me home. Sometimes we sat in the car for a couple of minutes. He would go to work and come over when he got off. I could hear him coming a mile away. I would be lying in bed and hear the music blasting. "Here comes Mike," I would say with a smile.

Our relationship was short, but it was good. We spent a lot of time together. We laughed, we talked about our futures, we had deep conversations. We didn't argue; we understood one another on a different level. It was different! We meshed. I think we would have lasted longer if circumstances hadn't changed, or should I say if *my* circumstances hadn't changed. Every day I came home from school and took a nap; that was something I did since starting school. It was routine for me. I walked to and from school with friends, sometimes, so I just assumed that I was tired.

In February, I started noticing that I would be out of breath by the time I got home. The walk home from school was the same, but it seemed longer. It sometimes felt like I jogged home. The feeling of exhaustion didn't scare me, but it grabbed my attention. One day, I was lying in bed, thinking about nothing, when it occurred to me that I missed my period—twice. I got out of bed and went outside to get some air. I saw my friend who lived across the street. I needed to talk to someone. I needed to say it out loud, so I told her. I was nervous. I was not sure what was going on. I went to school the next day and spoke to the nurse. I told her I missed two periods. It was almost March.

She told me I might be pregnant. I looked at her like she had two heads.

She instructed, "Listen, get a pill bottle, and wash it well. Then, when you have your first pee in the morning, pee in the pill bottle. You don't have to fill it, but I need the first part to see what's going on."

I couldn't focus for the rest of the day. I must have had a distraught look on my face because everyone was asking me what was wrong. I didn't reply. I was thinking about my escape or how I was going to run away because my mom had talked to me time and time again about getting pregnant, so I knew what the outcome might be.

That day I got home from school, I didn't take a nap. I just laid in the bed asking, "Lord, what have I done?"

I got up to wash out the pill bottle and set it in a safe place to let it dry as instructed. Once I finished, I went outside because I had friends over. The next morning, I got up and peed in the pill bottle. I secured the pill bottle and tucked it into my purse. I went to school with a heavy heart, full of worry. First period I didn't go to the clinic because I wasn't ready for anything the nurse had to say. I didn't think that I was pregnant because I didn't have any morning sickness. All I could think about was that I was in my junior year of high school, and I couldn't afford to slip like that. Third period came, and I knew it was time to go to the clinic.

I walked in, and she asked for the pill bottle. With hesitation, I gave it to her and stood there. She took out some type of strip from a container. With each action, my anxiety grew. She put the strip inside the bottle and took a small dropper to put urine on the rest of the strip. It was a pregnancy test strip. Within seconds she looked at me and calmly said, "Yes, you're pregnant."

I started backing up in disbelief. I backed up all the way into the wall. When my back hit the wall, the tears started uncontrollably streaming down my cheeks. I stood there for a minute, then I slid down the wall, slowly, with my heart sinking deeper and deeper into my chest. I hit the floor, crying, like someone close to me had just died. I couldn't contain myself.

She looked at me from across the desk. "I'm sorry. I can tell your mom with you."

I tried to look at her through my tears and found my breath because, like the time at the water park, I couldn't breathe.

"I have to do this on my own."

"Don't wait too long because you need care. "

I made my way out of the clinic and found my friend, the girl from across the street who I first told that I hadn't had a cycle in a couple of months. I told her what the school nurse said, then I told Vallerie. I didn't take a nap after school that day. I called Tweety and told him that I was pregnant.

"It ain't mine. You better tell Antoine!" Those were his words.

I wanted to punch him through the phone. I was dumbfounded. I couldn't understand what he was saying because this was supposed to be the guy who loved me and was always there. When he uttered those words, I instantly hated him. When I needed him the most, he turned his back on me. All the seeds that I tried to smother, so that they would die, fully bloomed in that very moment. There was a new, deeper, more embedded level of hurt, rejection, abandonment, confusion, and fear. That was my garden. The roots had attached to my heart and the weeds grew, removing everything that I was fighting for to be my life. Love, joy, happiness, acceptance, and confidence. It felt like a cactus had grown where my heart used to be. I was paralyzed and bleeding from the heart. I hated myself.

My thoughts started to run rapid. *How did I let this happen to me? Why did I go with him that day? I thought he loved me. What am I going to do? Who's going to be here for me now? Why the -\*- would he do me this way? Antoine! Really! Call Antoine! That's what this n\*gga tells* *me?* The more I thought, the angrier I became. I didn't want my mom to know, so I buried myself in my room because that was where I hid from the world, and I also found my best mask in there. My thoughts overwhelmed me and then, it dawned on me that I had to tell Mike. I didn't want to because I liked him.

Mike and I were talking while he was on his way to work. I disrupted the conversation.

"I need to tell you something."

"What is it?" His voice sounded leery.

Mike was moving quickly into my life as a long-term boyfriend; we were happy together. Although I don't believe in astrology, both of us were Virgos and it seemed that we knew one another as we knew ourselves. I started to cry softly because I didn't want to tell him. I said, "I'm pregnant."

There was a long pause, a stillness as we sat on the phone. I broke down crying.

"It's going to be alright. Stop crying! I will be over there when I get off work."

I was certain that he wasn't going to show up because our relationship was new. We were only three months in, so I wondered if he thought, "damn, is it mine?" Although we had protected sex every time, anything is possible. I was laying in the bed, and I heard music a few blocks over. I knew it was Mike because of the song he was playing. He was playing "I Wanna Know" by R&B singer, Joe. That was one of our songs. He came over after work as promised, and he greeted me with open arms. I laid my head on his chest as he wrapped his arms around me. The tears fell. This time I cried because I needed to feel love. When he held me in his arms, I felt for a second that everything was going to be alright. The guilt, shame, and anguish had all faded in that moment. I felt safe, the security of the hug made me feel a sense of protection from the mean world I was currently living in. When I was done crying, we leaned against his car and talked. He asked, "Is it mine?" I started to cry again. I answered, "No." The tears streamed down my cheeks. I wished it was at that moment.

He grabbed my hand, and encouraged me, "Let's sit in the car." We sat in the car to keep folks from seeing me sob. He was so patient with me. He listened to me reason with myself and my current situation. I was trying to make sense of the whole thing. As we talked through the minutes of the day, he gained an understanding of my brokenness. That night I let him in a little bit more.

Then he asked the million-dollar question. "Have you told your mom?"

I raised my head and looked over at him. "No." He wiped the tears from my eyes.

"I will tell her." He calmly spoke.

I told him, "No, I will tell her. Just give me some time."

"Okay, I am giving you a couple of days, and if you don't tell her, I will because you need care."

Every night we talked, and he would ask, "Did you tell her?"

The answer was always, "No, not yet."

He was adamant, "Okay, tell her by tomorrow or I'm going to tell her."

That night I cried myself to sleep. The next morning when she came to wake me up, as she turned to walk out, I said, "Ma!"

She turned around.

"I have something to tell you."

"What is it?"

I propped myself up, dropped my head and said, "I'm pregnant." Big teardrops fell onto my hand one after another. Then, I looked up at her with tears streaming down my face.

Without a word, she looked at me and walked

away. I got up and started dressing for school. She came back into my room and said, "You're staying home today."

Strangely, I didn't feel like I was going to die that day. I laid back in the bed, staring at the ceiling. Later that morning, Momma came back and said, "Let's talk."

I got up and followed her lead. We walked through the dining room into the kitchen where I thought we were going to talk, but she kept going.

We sat on the back steps of the house.

"Who is the daddy?"

"Tweety."

She dropped her head in disappointment. "Okay," well we need to schedule a doctor's appointment."

"For what, Ma? I don't want no baby!"

She looked at me and said, "Well, you got one! And an abortion isn't an option."

She called and made an appointment. Her, my aunt Emma, and I went to the appointment at Lee Davis clinic. I hoped that something magical was going to happen like when I took the test, I was not going to be pregnant. The lady gave me a cup to pee in. I peed in the cup; she tested the urine.

"Yes, you are pregnant." She said it with such ease.

I was mad because I already knew that. I thought *This lady is stupid! We know that. That's why I'm here, Miss.*

She told my mom that I also had a yeast infection. She gave me some cream and told me to apply it and to be careful to not insert it because it could cause a miscarriage. Once I had the cream, I thought it would be an uncomplicated way to miscarry. I got home, showered, and the first thing I did was insert the cream. I used it for seven days and nothing happened. My mom found me an OB-GYN doctor—Dr. Szeja. This man was a gift from God. He was the most thoughtful and gentle doctor. He was what I needed.

When I first met him, he wasn't my favorite because he had to examine me and do all the necessary things for an initial visit. Then he ordered blood work. *BLOOD WORK!* Was this necessary? All I could think was *this man doesn't like me, and he is punishing me because I will be a teen mom.* I was terrified of needles, so I hated shots. I cried when my mom agreed to take me for blood work. She knew this about me, and she agreed anyway. I was certain that this was a form of punishment. I was so upset about being pregnant that I cried every day for two months. Everything made me cry.

A few weeks into knowing that I was pregnant, Mike decided that he didn't want to be with me anymore. It hurt, but somehow, I knew it was coming. I didn't want to understand because I was pregnant when we started seeing each other; I just didn't know it. When he broke up with me, I was upset, but I understood his reason for the breakup. After that, I knew that it was going to be a hard road. The next day, I called Tweety's mom and told her that I was pregnant, because my mom made me.

She said, "You are?"

"Yes"

"Did you tell Tweety?" she inquired.

"Yes, but he said that it's not his."

She was upset.

She told me that she would call me back. Next thing I knew the phone rang and it was Tweety. He cursed me out like a stranger on the street. The more he talked, I felt something raging on the inside of me. My hatred toward him started to grow at a rapid pace in my heart. I hated him and hated that I was pregnant by him. I wanted it to all disappear. I felt like I was in a nightmare. I hated life. I couldn't understand why this was happening to me. I still hadn't told everyone that I was pregnant. I was embarrassed.

One day Elijah came to see me while my mom and stepdad were headed out.

My dad said, "Are you going to leave them here?"

My mom said, "Yes, the damage is already done."

I ran to her with my finger over my mouth, indicating to her to be quiet. I hadn't told him yet. I didn't know how because he was the one that I never got over; we just drifted apart.

I was months pregnant, in bed, sad, and depressed often because I thought that my life was over. As I laid there in a daze one day, the phone rang. I answered it with all that I had. There was the deep Barry White voice on the other end asking to speak to me.

I said, "This is she." It was Kevin.

"What's up? I haven't really heard from you lately."

There was a pause, "I know. I have to tell you something."

I wanted to tell him so that he could leave my life, too, because Tweety and Mike had left.

He asked, "What is it?"

"I'm pregnant!" I started to cry again. I was so hurt by this that every time I thought about it or mentioned it, I would cry.

"I know; I was just waiting on you to tell me. Why are you crying?" His voice was so gentle.

"My life is over," I spoke through my tears.

"No, it isn't."

"It is."

"What did the daddy say?" Why did he have to ask that?

An instant rage of hate hit me, "He said that it isn't his."

Another pause. I cried because I was so angry. He said, "Listen, I don't know anything about being a father, but I will be there for you and help you any way that I can."

I felt a sense of relief, and that everything could be okay. My life wasn't over like I thought.

I was living life as best I could. It was junior year and things were great at school. It was when I got home reality set in day after day. With each day passing, I found myself hating Tweety more. I wanted him to die because he deceived me, and I felt alone. I made the best out of what I had. I went to school every day and very few people knew that I was pregnant because I didn't show much. I was glad because I was embarrassed to be pregnant at the age of 16. It was the end of the school year, and the seniors were having "Senior Skip Days." I went to as many of them as possible. My mom knew because I would always get permission. There was one I remembered the most. We all left school and went to Shoney's, a restaurant on Busch Boulevard to have breakfast. There had to be about 50 of us.

When we left the restaurant, we were headed to the beach, and it was raining. I was in the car with some friends, and there were about six people in the car. We were trailing one another; about ten cars altogether. We were going around a curve on the interstate, it was slippery, and a car started sliding across the road. The car I was in was sliding off the road, too, and it was headed into a pole at full speed. Our lives flashed before our eyes. The car stopped inches before crashing into the pole. Nothing, but God! Two of the other cars that were traveling with us crashed into one another.

We all got out the cars to get our thoughts together. We were so thankful for life. We checked on the two cars that crashed into one another. Thank God there weren't any life-threatening injuries. We were talking in the car afterwards and we talked about what we saw that flashed before our eyes. That was my last senior skip day with them. I never told my mom about that, but I was thankful to God that He saved us. That could have been a tragic story. I started to remember that more than me mattered now.

I started to think about life more seriously because it was about to get real for me. It was now summer, and I was due September 23, 1997. I had to start getting my life in order because I had a baby growing inside of me and I wasn't sure if I wanted him or if I was ready for the journey.

I had to attend summer school and that was when the assistant principal got wind that I was pregnant, and this lady hated me. Her name was Ms. Mays; I will never forget her.

She called me and my mom into the office to tell my mom that she should put me in McFarland School. That was a school for teen moms. She told my mom that I would be a bad influence on the other girls there at Hillsborough; and that most girls who got pregnant before graduating didn't graduate anyway. She said it would be a good thing for me to attend McFarland.

My mom said, "No, she is staying here, and she will graduate. Thank you, but no thank you! Plus, she wants to graduate with her class."

This lady really didn't want me at the school, but my momma stood her ground. I continued in summer school. One day, I was standing talking with friends and there were two boys playing. I was not paying attention while they were playing, one turned to run away and ran directly into me and my stomach. I was instantly angry and ready to fight. By that point, I hated all boys who tried to hurt me. I went home that day, and as I was sitting combing my niece's hair, I got a sharp pain from nowhere. I started screaming and my mom came running, "What's wrong?"

I said, "I don't know, but it hurts!!"

She called the doctor. He said, "Get her to the hospital."

I went to University Community Hospital Women's Center. They started doing all these things to me. I didn't understand what was going on. I was there for three days. That was the start of my blood pressure being out of control. I was in and out of the hospital the rest of the month of June. It was the fourth of July. I didn't like males, especially those who were close to me. I knew that they were going to leave me or hurt me, eventually.

We were at my grandfather's house having a bar-b-que and I wanted ice cream; I went to the store and purchased some. I got one for me and one to share with the others who were over there. I put them both in the freezer and I was intentional to make sure that everyone knew which was mine and which was the one to share.

I was very possessive during my pregnancy. Vallerie came over and I decided that I wanted some of *my* ice cream. I went to fix a bowl of the ice cream, and someone had eaten out of it. I was extremely UPSET! I started crying. My tears poured from rage. I started fussing to the top of my lungs because I wanted to know who ate *my* ice cream when I made it clear that it was mine. When I found out that it was my cousin's girlfriend's kids, I wanted to fight. I was upset with Joe. There was nothing that he could have said to me because I made it clear that it was MY ice cream and not to touch it. Vallerie was able to get me out of the house. We left the bar-b-que because I wanted to kill someone about ice cream.

I don't remember where we went before her house, but I ended up falling asleep at her house. Vallerie came to wake me up while on her couch saying, "Here, get the phone, it's your mom."

I thought that she was calling to check on me because it was like two in the morning and I was not home. Much to my surprise, she was calling to tell me that my older brother had been shot. I don't remember the conversation, but I knew that I needed to go to where she was because she didn't sound good.

I started crying and asked Val to take me to the hospital. When I got there, my mom was crying, and my uncles were enraged. She said to me that they couldn't find a pulse in his leg, and they may have to cut it off. I stopped breathing for a couple of seconds. My uncle Gene said, "Let's pray."

We started praying, but I was thinking, "why?" God hadn't been around in a while. I was so full of hate that I couldn't recognize God even when He was always present.

So, we prayed. While we were in prayer, they decided to call in a specialist. The specialist came in and was able to find a faint pulse and he said, "We can save the leg." My brother went into surgery and that was the longest wait ever! The next day, I called our dad and let him know that Weeba, my brother, had been shot and was in the hospital.

Shortly after that, I was back in the hospital for a day or two. My blood pressure was uncontrollable, it would shoot through the roof whenever I got upset and that was all the time. In that season of my life, I didn't like many people and I wanted to be in the world alone. The last time my pressure went up, it was because I was really upset. It didn't take much. My aunt said, "Come, let me take your pressure." I didn't want her to because I knew I was supposed to be on bed rest and not allowing myself to get upset.

I went across the street, and she took my pressure, and it was like 195 over 105, something like that. She instantly freaked out! Her being a nurse, she knew that that was too high. She made my mom call the doctor. It was during regular business hours, so the doctor said to her, "I will meet you all at the hospital at 5pm."

She called my uncle Gene and told him what was happening with me. He told her to let me sit in front of the fish tank and look at the fish swim. I grew angrier and my pressure was still going up. I thought, *why did I have to sit and look at these stupid fish, all they did was swim around the tank*. The more I thought about it, the madder I got. I sat there mad, watching the fish; and, before I knew it, I was calm, and my pressure started to go down. We went to the hospital, and I was admitted for another three days.

All summer long I was in and out of the hospital. Now, it was the end of July and things were still crazy with my pressure. I went to the doctor and things were out of order. He looked disappointed and concerned. He told my mom, "Meet me at the hospital at 6pm and pack your bags because you are staying. Because bed rest at home isn't working for you. You are endangering yourself and your child."

I went to the hospital on July 21st and when I left it was August 25th. I was on strict bed rest, the only thing I did was lay in bed on my right side or left side. I only sat up for 30 minutes a day. I couldn't leave my room at all. I could not take a shower unless the nurse was there with me. I wasn't allowed to sit at the table and look out the window. The walls in the hospital room were closing in on me. I got depressed, felt lonely, and I cried because I couldn't do anything. I wanted to know why this was happening to me. Was I being punished for becoming a teen mom? The hospital was terrifying for me. I barely slept because I would have nightmares. Nurses would come in my room at five in the morning to draw blood from me and I would have a fit because I hated needles. I would call and wake my mom up because I was scared. That was a hard 30 plus days to endure.

# Reflection page

What heartbreak did you endure that changed your life? How did you get through it?

_____

_____

_____

_____

_____

_____

_____

_____

_____

_____

_____

_____

_____

_____

_____

_____

# Reflection

_____

_____

_____

_____

_____

_____

_____

_____

_____

_____

_____

_____

_____

_____

_____

_____

_____

_____

_____

# TRYING TO FIND MY WAY
*(Where is He?)*

H ere I was in the hospital at 16 years old, hating life. There was no rhyme or reason to live. I would get visitors, mostly my mom, who came every day if she could. Elijah visited me often. He snuck me food and whatever I wanted because my diet was restricted. He would sit and talk with me for a while and make me laugh. He would always leave me with a smile on my face. His visits were always bittersweet. I was glad when he came and sad when it was time for him to go. He did what he could while he was there to uplift my spirits.

I was in a dark state of mind. My uncle Gene came to see me, and I thought that he could tell that life was escaping me and I didn't want to fight anymore. I just wanted everything to be over. I had been there so long that the nurses started to mistreat me. Like I mentioned earlier, I couldn't leave the bed. I had to depend on the nurses for everything. To depend on anyone was hard for me, especially during that time. I would call for juice and they would bring me one or two, four-ounce juices as if that were enough. One day, while my favorite nurse, Lisa Hart, an angel, was off from work, I felt the difference in care, sharply. Nurse Hart took care of me, and she made me feel loved. Well, the day she wasn't there, and I called for something to drink—no response. I waited 30 minutes and called again. No one ever came. My doctor, Dr. Szeja, came while doing his daily check in, he noticed that my blood pressure was high. I was upset. No, I was angry because they wouldn't bring me anything to drink, and I was frustrated that I couldn't get it myself. So, he asked what was wrong and the tears started to flow. I explained to him what happened and that I was frustrated because I could not walk, and I really didn't need those dumb nurses. On this visit he came with the specialist. They looked at one another, then he said, "Excuse us a minute." They walked out and I'm not sure what they talked about or said to the nurses, but I didn't have any more issues after that. All their behaviors toward me changed. They all became helpful and caring of my needs.

Tweety came to see me once while I was in the hospital, and he caused my blood pressure to go up so high that they asked him to leave, and I let them know that I didn't want him to come back. We were in mid-August and things weren't getting better. They had discovered that my baby wasn't growing; I was scheduled for an amniocentesis to see what was going on. An amniocentesis was where they took this extremely long needle and stuck it in your stomach down into the amniotic sac to take fluid. Once they ran the tests on the fluid, they learned that my baby lungs weren't developed. By that period in the pregnancy his lungs should have been developed. He explained to me that I would have to get two steroid shots to increase the development of his lungs. He wasn't growing and his lungs weren't developing. I became afraid. This was where we weren't sure that he was going to make it. My blood pressure issues became the second problem because the health of the baby took precedence, of course. They started treating my baby. A few days later, Uncle Gene came and brought a case of T.D. Jakes cassette tapes for me to listen to. I was thinking, *who is T.D. Jakes?* And what did he have to say to me that was going to make me feel better. I listened to a couple of tapes, and I didn't understand what he was talking about. I knew what he was talking about, but I didn't understand. I could still feel life slipping away from me and I was losing all hope for life. Days seemed dark and nights even darker. My mother and nurse knew that I was becoming depressed. I didn't call mom as much; I didn't smile or talk much. I cried most of the time. I was tired of laying in that bed, not being able to do anything. The social worker arranged the opportunity for me to do arts and crafts in my hospital bed. I could only sit up for 30 minutes at a time, so some projects that I worked on took me a few days and it kept me occupied. The visits became exceedingly rare with everyone else, but the visits from my mom never stopped.

My Aunt Minnie, who lived in North Carolina, got word about what was going on with me and she came to Florida. She came to see me, and we talked. My auntie was the only person other than my uncle Gene that I knew had a deep relationship with something spiritual. I didn't know what to call it, but I knew that it was something special. She prayed for me and that was that. I think it was the very next day my Aunt Minnie and uncle Gene came walking into the room. In my uncle's hand there was a bag. In that bag was a gift for me. I was excited, I was 16 and they had a gift for me. I remember him pulling this book out of the bag. It was a Bible. I was thinking, *a Bible?* I was confused as to why he wanted to give me a Bible, but okay. When I looked at the Bible, I liked it a lot. My name was engraved on it in silver writing and the Bible was navy blue. I smiled because it was personalized just for me. So, as they stood at the bed, and we talked, my uncle asked me if I knew what it meant to be saved. I told him no. They proceeded to explain to me what it meant. My aunt asked if I wanted to be saved and I told them yes. So, on that day, August 18, 1997, I accepted Christ as my Savior.

One funny memory about the hospital was I used to have sleepovers. My oldest brother's girlfriend was pregnant, too. So, she would spend the night with me. Those moments gave me life, I had someone to laugh and talk with. Someone that seemed to understand and had empathy for me. We would order out, the whole nine yards like we were at home. I appreciate what she did for me. I know she may not remember, but it meant a lot to me. My own brother never came to see me while I was in the hospital.

As days went on, things weren't changing with my health and the baby still wasn't growing. We were now at Week 20. I was being monitored more closely because things were declining with me and the baby. The doctor told my mom that they could only leave him in there a few more days, and they were going to have to induce labor. I looked at her and asked, "What that meant?" She said, "They will give you meds to make you go into labor so that you can have the baby." *Cool! I was ready to get this over.*

On August 21ˢᵗ my life started on a journey that I would forever remember. That morning the inducing started. The requirements were to not have eaten anything after midnight the night before. So, the last time I ate was about 10 o'clock that night. Early morning, we started the process. I thought that it would be over soon. By noon, nothing had happened. I was getting a little antsy because I was hungry and could not have anything except ice chips. By five o'clock nothing had happened so I thought I could finally eat. NOPE! I still had to wait. Dr. Szeja came in and checked me and said, "You haven't dilated at all. We will leave you on for another couple of hours and see what happens." Now my blood pressure was starting to go up and down because I was frustrated out of my mind, and I was VERY hungry. I was hooked up to the monitors and the readings were off the charts because I was over it and I just wanted to be left alone. By nine thirty that night nothing happened, so he finally said, "Okay let's take her off and feed them." I felt like it was Christmas! I don't remember what I ate, but I was happy.

He came back about ten thirty and said, "Okay, we will try again tomorrow. Nothing to eat or drink after midnight." I ate all I could before then. I went to sleep once I was full. The next morning, they came to wake me to start the process again. On that morning we started a little earlier, it was about seven o'clock instead of eight. So, things got on their way. I knew that I couldn't eat or drink, so I went back to sleep after they did everything that was needed. The entire time I was sleeping I could hear the baby monitor and feel my stomach tightening and releasing. By 10 o'clock the nurse woke me up and she asked, "Do you feel the contractions that you are having?"

I asked, "What do contractions feel like? I feel tightening; that's all."

While I was speaking, she said, "You are having a contraction right now." With a surprised face she asked, "You don't feel that?!"

I replied "Nope" as I closed my eyes to rest because I didn't want to talk anymore. I wanted to eat. She called my mom and the doctor. About noon the specialist came in. He asked, "How are you?"

And I replied, "I don't know."

He then said, "I see that you are having contractions now so hopefully it won't be long."

My mom came and she said, "Are you ready?"

I replied, "Ready for this to be over so I can go home."

It was August 22nd. The contractions were non-stop, and I felt nothing. The doctor came in and checked me and noted that I had finally dilated a centimeter. Now I was two centimeters dilated. We thought the induced labor was progressing smoothly. It was now five o'clock and we were still monitoring and watching the huge contractions that I didn't feel and watching the baby's heartbeat. What's happening? NOTHING! Nothing was happening. I was having contraction after contraction, and nothing was happening. I was hungry and frustrated, around eight o'clock my pressure started to rise again. The doctor came in confused because he couldn't understand how I was having such bad contractions and I didn't feel them, and I was not dilating. He said, "Let's stop it so she can eat, and we will reconvene tomorrow." Once I was unplugged from everything,

I ate until I couldn't eat anymore. He came back and said, "See you tomorrow." After I ate, I talked with my mom for a while then I went to sleep. Those two days were long and exhausting.

August 23rd, I woke up early and they started the process. It was so early in the morning, and I was TIRED. I was tired of everything. So, I woke up angry. As I lay in the bed, I felt numb. I was not talking to anyone because I felt like I was being punished for my mistake. And I was hurt to my heart because the person that helped make this baby wasn't there with me and I felt like, what had I done to myself. I was having contractions and still not feeling any pain. I just laid there and watched the monitors, and my eyes would fill with tears, and I would cry softly so that no one could hear me. On that day, my mom, grandma, godmother, and god sister were there. They talked and waited for something to happen because they felt that day was the day. I started going into labor. So, I was moved to labor and delivery, and I had dilated another centimeter. Now I was at three centimeters dilated and it was early, so yes it was happening that day.

By three that afternoon nothing further happened. I laid there looking at the monitors as my eyes filled with tears again. I was hungry, tired, and I wanted to give up. I felt life was once again leaving my body. This time as I cried softly, they heard me. My mom noticed I was crying. Before she could ask what was wrong, I lost it. My mom started crying too, then my godmother, and my grandma. As they tried to console me, the doctor came in and noticed how distraught I was. My blood pressure was rising. He said, "We have to keep her calm to get her blood pressure down." By evening—still nothing.

I said to my god sister who was sitting with me, "I have to pee."

She asked, "Do you want me to help you to the restroom?"

I told her, "Yes." I was exhausted and weak. I felt numb. On my way to the restroom, liquid started to run down my legs. So, I stopped walking and they called for the nurse because they were sure that my water had broken. The nurse came in and helped me back to bed.

The nurse checked me and advised us, "She hasn't dilated anymore, but I'm going to call the doctor."

Dr. Szeja decided that he would force my water to break since it had not, although I was losing fluid.

He said, "We are going to increase the dosage of meds and that should help her dilate."

Hours passed. My water was broken, but I still hadn't dilated. I was having contractions. I felt myself getting weaker. My pressure was rising higher and higher. Things started to get scary for me. About 8:15pm, the doctor said "I have to take this baby now! He is stuck in the birth canal and she's not dilating. His heart rate is dropping."

I looked at my mom, her face was pale, and she looked terrified. I didn't know what was going on, but I knew it wasn't good.

He told her, "I am calling for the anesthesiologist now. We have to get the baby out of there because it's not looking good."

Within minutes, the anesthesiologist was there. He said, "I'm here to do your epidural." He explained to me what it was and said, "Let's get started."

My mom remarked, "Wait, I'm leaving."

My god sister said, "Me, too."

My grandma said, "I can't stay for that."

They all left. He looked at my godmother and asked, "Ma'am?"

She said, "I'm not leaving my baby."

My 16-year-old brain was in overload. I was scared out of my mind. He turned me on my side and advised that there would be a small pinch. He inserted the needle, as he tried to go along the spine, he could not. So, he had to remove the needle.

He said, "I'm going to have to sit you up." He sat me up and turned me to the side of the bed with my legs hanging off. He asked my godmother to sit in front of me to keep me still and calm.

She sat in front of me and stared me in my eyes and said, "You are going to be all right." As she said this, I felt another small pinch.

As he tried to run it along the spine, he was unable to. He removed the needle again. And he said, "There is something blocking it."

My godmother replied, "So what do we need to do?"

I started to cry.

He said, "We are going to try one more time. Bend forward as far as you can." He asked my godmother to hold my shoulders forward. As I sat there cradled forward and tears roll down my cheeks, he said, "A small pinch." This time he was able to get the needle to go along the spine. He cleaned me up and laid me down.

He said "I'm sorry, it never takes that much. You are a strong young lady. Good luck."

He walked out. I looked at my godmother with confusion and hurt on my face and she said, "You are going to be all right."

The nurses came in and wheeled me into the operating room. When I got there, my mom was in one of the operation outfits. Things started to go blank for me from there.

I remembered someone asking me, "Can you feel that?"

I laid there wondering was my life over. I felt tugging and pulling with a sense of urgency. And the next thing I heard was crying. I was lying there, and I heard crying. I felt no emotions. I was numb. They brought the baby to me, but I just glanced at him. They took him away and my mom went with them. The next thing I remembered was being in recovery. I stared at the roof until I fell asleep.

I don't know how long I was asleep, but I remembered my mom waking me. She said, "He looks just like Tweety." I looked at her blankly. She said, "You may as well let Tweety see the baby." I shrugged my shoulders and closed my eyes. When she left, tears rolled down the sides of my face. I was angry. I was angry because of everything. Not just one thing, but everything.

I didn't realize that my life and my baby's life was saved. They finally came and rolled me into my room. There were six or more people in my room. The baby was there. Tweety had red roses in his hands. I looked at him and looked away. Momma started to talk to him. He washed his hands, and she gave him the baby. I could only hear all this because I wouldn't look at him. When she gave him the baby, he started to cry. I looked at him and looked away with anger in my heart. The room started to clear out and things started to settle. I looked in the baby bed and saw the baby and as I looked at him, I thought to myself, my life had changed, and I was only 16. I laid there in silence, while the others were talking. They thought that I was sleeping. Tweety and Tonja were getting ready to go and he leaned over the bed and kissed my forehead. I thought to myself, *I hate him.*

On August 23, 1997, I became a mother. The next day my mom came to the hospital and the baby wasn't in the room.

She asked, "Where is the baby?" I shrugged my shoulders. She called the nurse's station and Lisa (the same nurse I mentioned earlier on) was there.

Lisa answered, "I have him. I will bring him in."

She brought him into the room and Momma was ready to hold him. She asked me, "Have you held him at all?" I shook my head no. She then asked if I wanted to hold him, and I shook my head no, again. She said, "This is your baby, and he needs your love."

We had visitors all day long as I was in and out of sleep. Dr. Szeja visited and asked how I was feeling. He increased the pain medicines because I was in extreme pain.

The next day, August 24th, the nurse came in and said, "Okay, we have to get you up and moving."

I said, "It's six o'clock in the morning."

She said, "I know, I let you sleep in…"

I thought, *you let me sleep in!*

She said, "Let's start with a shower." I tried to stand up and I thought that I was going to die. "One step at a time," she stated. When I was in the shower, the water started to run down my body and once my bandages were soaked, she said, "Okay, we are going to take your bandages off."

She then pulled the bandage off and I looked down and all I saw were stitches and staples. I didn't realize that I had major surgery with stitches and staples which kept me together. I washed myself and she cleaned my wound. After I was done with the shower, she sat me in a chair while they finished making my bed. Fresh clean sheets and back into the bed I went. She asked if I wanted the baby to come in, I shrugged my shoulders again. She brought him in, and I just stared at him. It was time for his feeding, and she asked if I wanted to feed him, and I told her no. She took him with her and fed him.

About noon, I woke up and my mom was there, and she had the baby. I told her that I wasn't feeling well. She felt me and I had a fever, so she asked the nurse to call the doctor. The doctor ordered antibiotics to ward off infection.

I asked my mom, "How did you get the baby?"

She replied, "Oh, he was at the nurses' station when I got here." She held him, talked to him, changed him, and loved on him.

The doctor said I couldn't hold him until my fever broke. I was okay with that. It had now been three days since he was born, and I hadn't held him yet. The night had come, and Momma went home.

The nurse came in and asked, "Do you want me to take him to the nursey?"

I looked at her, then him and said, "No, you can leave him."

So, she moved him closer to the bed because my motion was limited by the pain. I laid there and stared at him for a while. Then, I decided to hold him. I took him out of the bed and held him in my arms. I released this deep sigh, and it seemed like all my emotions returned to my body at that time. I was in love. That was when I really looked at my baby for the first time.

The next morning the doctor came in and I was asleep with him in my arms. He said, "Guess who's going home today if the lab work comes back well."

I smiled. For the first time in weeks, I smiled. Welp, when the test results came back, I was still feverish, and there was an infection. Dr. Szeja said, "I don't know about sending you home."

The waterworks started. I was so sad that I couldn't go home. I don't know what happened, but a while later he said that I could go home. That was one of the happiest days of my life. When I went home, reality started to set in. I WAS A MOM. I was 16 years old and a mom. Because I had always been around babies, taking care of him wasn't going to be hard, at least I thought it wouldn't be. I quickly realized that babysitting and parenting are two different things. I was on mama duty 24 hours a day, seven days a week.

Everyone thought "oh, you're young and your mom will do most of the work." HA! My mom helped me when I first came home because I was sick, weak, and had a fever. However, she made sure that I made no mistake about my responsibility. Sick and all, I was a **MOTHER,** and she was going to make sure I understood that.

I would look at my four pounds, eight-ounce baby and I realized, he was really mine. The more I spent time with him, the more I loved him. He was so small and fragile, but he was a fighter! Thinking about all the things he endured in the womb and the neglect of his mother's touch, during his first few days on earth, could have given him a reason to give up. Watching how strong he was as a little guy made me want to get better for him. I made sure I took care of myself for him.

As I got better, I was anxiously waiting to return to school. It was my senior year. It was mid-September when I returned to school. Everything was in full swing. I WAS READY! Tenth and eleventh grade were fun times. I knew that my senior year was going to be LIFE! I went to school almost every day. As strong as my little guy was, he wasn't strong enough to be illness free. Due to his lung development issues, he had asthma, and it wasn't kind to him. So, we would have doctor's appointments often. My mom would not take him to the doctor, it was my job.

I was a part of the it-crowd, I wanted to participate in everything. Well, Jeanette, my mom, had a bit of reality to teach me. My son slept with me every night. He woke up every two hours for a feeding. I was the one getting up making bottles, feeding him, burping him, changing him throughout the night. People asked me how I could fall asleep so fast, sleep for 30 minutes, and wake up like I had slept all night. I got plenty of practice from those crazy, a-little-sleep-here-and-there nights. My mom would get my son every morning at six when she opened the doors of her home childcare center. My time to wake up for school was six thirty in the morning. So, from six o'clock to six thirty I got the best sleep. There were nights that I would fall asleep feeding my baby and wake up right away because I felt myself drifting off. There were nights that I was so upset with him because he wouldn't sleep. I would cry and beg him to just sleep for a few more minutes. Some nights were better than others. My "everyday naps" after school ended. I would get one in every now and then. I was 17 and such a parent. If I were later than usual getting home, my mom would page me. My beeper would go off and I knew I had to go, without even looking at the pager. If you don't know what a pager is…Google it!

Everywhere I went, my son went. If the weather was nice, I took him with me. So, we went to football games, basketball games, and Senior Skip Days.

Momma would say, "Oh, where you going? Take your baby, let me get him dressed for you."

He was my side kick. I must tell the truth; I was glad when the weather wasn't good because Momma would keep him. I was 17, a single parent, and a senior in high school. I thought things couldn't get any worse.

My brother's girlfriend randomly asked me one day, "You still talk to Mike?"

I said, "No, not really. I miss him though."

She said, "I think he talks to your friend across the street."

I said "What?!"

"I saw her leave with him a couple of times at night."

I was angry. Because she knew how I felt about him. I shared everything with her because I felt like we were cousins. She came over one day, and we were sitting on the porch.

She said, "I have something to tell you." I looked at her. She said, "I slept with Mike."

I said, "What Mike?"

She replied, "Yours."

I looked at her. I wanted to fight her, but I didn't. I knew that our friendship was over. She betrayed me. I haven't spoken to her from that day in 1997 to this day. I was hurt. I couldn't believe that she had done that to me. So, not only were males hurting me. Females were hurting me, too. I was so angry with Mike and her that I couldn't bring myself to trust anyone.

Just like that, it was time to move again. We moved into my great grandmother's house. The same house I used to go to when I was in the sixth grade.

# LOVE IS BLIND

Life was happening, but it was good, and I was managing the best that I knew how. I had learned how to ignore my feelings, well, I learned to bury them. I still dream about my grandmother's house sometimes. That was where life started taking another turn for me. I was dating Kevin—in my mind. I had let him into my heart. We hung out, went on dates, and acted as if we were a couple, so I was convinced that we were.

I will never forget; it was Christmas of 1997 and his girlfriend came home for a visit. I thought that relationship was over. Much to my surprise, it wasn't. While she was home, they were hanging out. I was pushed to the back burner and didn't know why at the time. I received a phone call from one of my friends who told me that they saw Kevin and the girl in the mall. I was devastated! I thought that they were over, and I was his girl. NOPE. A few days passed and I had not heard from him. When he finally came over, I confronted him about what I had heard as we sat in his truck talking. He didn't hesitate to say, "Yeah, we were…that's my girlfriend. You wanna know what I bought her?"

I was speechless. My eyes filled with tears, and I got out of his truck without a word. I didn't slam the door or anything, I just got out and walked into the house. He called out for me, but I kept walking as if I didn't hear him. As the tears rolled down my cheeks and my heart started to remember the pain of being broken, I held my son close. He was a few months old, so his love was so pure for me. The next day, I decided that I would just live my life without a boyfriend. I started reconnecting with old friends and made new friends. Guys that I wouldn't talk to before, I started to befriend. I didn't tell Kevin, but things were at a good balance for me. When he wasn't there, someone else was. Things were what they were with us.

I remembered Elijah was home from college and he reached out to me. It was cool because he was a good person to me. He needed help with a paper he was writing for one of his classes over Spring Break, so I told him to come over. He came over and we were working on his paper. We still had a connection, and the attraction was there, but we maintained a friends-only relationship. I would never tell him what I was going through because I didn't want him to paint a picture of me.

He wasn't a man of many words, so I often didn't know what he was thinking; but there was always something about his eyes and the way he looked at me. It was like he knew how I felt and what I was going through. Well, as we sat and worked on the paper, Kevin showed up. He showed up unannounced, and I wasn't bothered. He came in and saw Elijah. He didn't say anything, but his face said *everything*. I continued to work with Elijah on his paper.

Kevin said to me, "Can I talk to you?"

I left Elijah's side; Kevin and I went to talk. We talked in his truck for about 10 minutes. I don't remember what was said, but he left, and he was upset. I didn't care because I remembered his "that's my girlfriend" comment. And it was a tit-for-tat moment, still it worked perfectly. I went back inside the house.

Elijah looked at me and asked, "I didn't get you in trouble, did I?"

I looked at him and said, "No."

A few days later, Elijah returned to school and Kevin, and I got back on track, at least I thought.

Weeks later, I paged Kevin. He didn't return my call. I paged him again. He called back. But something didn't sit well with me when he called back. So, I decided to use the phone feature code *67 to see where he called from, and I dialed the number.

The recording said "Thank you for calling _____ hotel…" I hung up. I started blowing up his pager. What the hell was he doing at the hotel and with who? Somehow, I ended up talking to the girl he was at the hotel with. I was in total disbelief. Weeks passed and everything was okay with me, but my trust in anything was out the door. I thought God sent him to me, and he would do me like this. There is no way that I wanted this God thing or anything serious with Kevin. But once again, I looked over what had happened and gave it another chance. I thought we were back on track.

My senior year was winding down, and school was everything that I needed it to be. A place to forget my reality. Outside of school was where the drama was. At home and in my relationships. Things were so unsettling for me that I was trying to find peace within. Sometime, before all of this, I heard a song by gospel artist Kirk Franklin called, "Why We Sing." I fell in love with that song. The first time I heard it, it just pulled my heart strings. I remember having my mom go to multiple flea markets to find that cassette tape with that song. Back then it was most popular to purchase songs on cassette, not CDs, or by download. We searched until we found it. I was originally looking for the single, but we found the whole album instead. I fell in love with the whole tape, so it was something that I would listen to often to keep my spirits up. I thought to myself, I will get back to Kevin and that drama in a minute.

My oldest brother and I still didn't see eye to eye. I was still convinced that he hated me. We argued all the time. He was so filled with anger after he was shot. It was like he was mad at the world but took it out on a few people. The house we lived in had one bathroom (I know that sounds ancient to some of you… LOL), so it was normal for more than one person to be in a bathroom at one time. So, his girlfriend was doing her hair and I had to tinkle. She said to come in, I went inside to sit on the toilet. My brother and I were arguing about something, I don't remember about what because we argued so much. He came in and pushed me off the toilet, I almost fell into the tub. I was crying and terribly angry, not to mention humiliated.

My mom started to curse and yell at him for what he had done to me. Once I got myself together, I put on my favorite mask again, the "I'm okay mask." I went into the bedroom and started listening to the Kirk Franklin tape. Listening to the words of each song helped me to know that there had to be more to life than hurt. Though, it seemed that every corner I turned, hurt was waiting on me.

We had about 15 days left as seniors. Kevin would pick me up most days from school. So again, I thought that we were a couple. Well, I found out that after he picked me up from school and dropped me home, he went to pick up someone else.

****

One Friday he picked me up from school. He took me home and we talked for a little while. He left. I hadn't heard from him the rest of the day which was kind of unusual. It was nighttime and I was giving my baby a bath. I paged him and he called back, this time from his cellphone. We talked, but something didn't sit well with me. So, I called the hotel from before. I asked for his room and the operator said, "One moment please." My heart sunk; it felt like I had taken a blow to my lungs. The phone started to ring, and my heart was beating 99 beats per minute. I hoped it couldn't be. *This couldn't be.* The third or fourth ring, he answered. My heart was heavy. I instantly filled with rage, and I said, "I will be there in a minute."

I asked my brother's girlfriend to watch my baby and called my best friend, Vallerie. I told her what happened, and she said, "I'm on my way."

While she was on her way, I put on my t-shirt, shorts, and sneakers. I was ready to fight. I didn't know who I was going to fight, but I knew it was someone. Him or her but I knew I needed to release some of the anger that was living on the inside of me. She didn't live far from me, so it didn't take her long to get to my house. When she got there, I hopped in the car, and we left. I never told my mom where I was going, just that I would be back, and Aja was watching the baby. When we got to the hotel, Kevin was walking to his truck. I jumped out of the car, and walked up to him enraged, ready for whatever. We were arguing. We were so loud that people were looking out their car windows and doors and the hotel. I cursed him out. As we went back and forth, he dropped the boom.

He said, "You not my girlfriend!" He climbed in this truck, closed the door, and left. I walked through the parking lot over to Val's car and got in. Val and I were about to leave the hotel when I thought, *he left by himself.*

I said, "He's not by himself. He left that b*tch upstairs." So, we backed into a parking space where we could see the hotel room he was in. I knew the room number because when the operator connected me, she gave me the room number. We sat and we talked; I was angry. She was always the reasonable one. I said to her, "I can't believe this!" This n***** tried me."

Before I could get that out good, a head popped out the curtain. I looked at Vallerie and said, "That's Kenya West!"

I jumped out of the car. I was furious. I was cursing and wildly irrational. I ran up the stairs and to the door with Vallerie right behind me trying to keep me calm. I knocked on the door. She didn't answer.

I said loudly, "I know you are in there, Kenya West, so open the f-ing door." She opened the door and saw the crazy look on my face. I asked in a calm voice, "What are you doing here with Kevin?"

She said, "We was going to go to the movies, but the movie wasn't starting yet."

So, I said to her, "I'm going to ask you a question, and I'm going to turn my back when I ask you this."

I turned around to face the parking lot because all of this was happening outside the room on the front balcony.

I asked, "Did you sleep with him?" (Not in those words).

She said "No."

I grumbled, "Don't f-ing lie to me."

Kenya was calm. "No, we just got here."

I turned around and walked past her into the hotel room. I looked around the room looking for evidence that they had either slept together, or they didn't. As I scanned the room, I noticed the bed was messed up, but it was clearly from them either sitting or lying on it.

Because we were classmates, we started to talk. She started to share with me about her and Kevin. So, while I thought that he was doing wonderful things for me, he was doing things for her as well. While we were talking, he paged her. She said, "That's him."

I said, "Call him back," so she did.

He asked if I was still there, she told him, "No. She left."

Val and I went back downstairs to sit in the car because he told Kenya that he would be back. I wanted to catch him in the room. I was furious, but

I didn't cry. He pulled into the parking lot. As he was backing in, about to park, he spotted Val's car and us sitting in it. He zoomed out of the parking lot almost hitting Val's car. We went back up to the room and sat with Kenya and waited for him to call or page her, but he did neither.

By the end of the night, we were the ones to take her home. I thought everything was cool and I was going to leave what happened over the weekend alone. It didn't need to get back to school, for what? Well, I was wrong again! Always giving people the benefit of the doubt. Kenya went back to school talking about it and how she was going to beat my ass. When I got wind of it, I was angry. I left class and I went on a hunt around the school looking for her, because if she was going to beat my ass, we would make it happen. That was my mind set.

I couldn't find her ANYWHERE! It was the end of the day; the last bell had just rung. Kevin and his friend came up to the school, it wasn't usual for them. I wasn't talking to Kevin, but I would talk to his friend because he was a mutual friend. I was telling him what had happened at school and how I was upset. I didn't know where Kevin was, and I didn't care. Kevin's friend, Val, and I were walking down the hall when I spotted Kenya. My heart started racing, and the rage returned. I started walking down the hallway toward her. I couldn't wait to get to her so, I started yelling, "Oh, you are going around the school telling people that you were going to beat me."

I briskly walked toward her.

I got madder by the moment. When we got close, Kenya said, "No, I didn't say that."

She was with a friend of hers and the friend blabbed, "Yes, you did."

I started cursing her out, ready to launch at her. Kevin's friend picked me up from behind and carried me out the door and said, "It's not worth it. You have 10 days left of school; you don't need to be suspended." He told Kevin, "Take her home."

I walked away and went to get into the car with Val. I was furious. I mean, if I could blow smoke out my ears and nose, it would have happened that day. I was so done with Kevin. I didn't want to be bothered with him anymore. I started to not care about anything or anyone. I decided to not let him in my heart or mind anymore. I was doing what I wanted from that moment. He had let me down too many times. I was done trying to get close to him. He had more than one person he was seeing at the time, in the same graduating class. That was why he couldn't take me to my prom, and prom was great! I was gorgeous. Thanks to my friend. There were so many guys that I pushed off for Kevin because I thought that he was serious about me. Silly me!

There was a guy at school that had a mad crush on me. But I wouldn't pay him much attention because we were in the same grade, and I liked older guys. However, he started to grow on me, and we became friends. We spent a lot of our senior year together because we had four classes together. He had worked a Publix since his ninth-grade year. So, he always brought me something to school. He knew what my favorite snacks were and what I liked to eat. So, most mornings he would bring me something to first period and that always made my day. But I wouldn't tell him because I had to keep up my image (LOL). But I liked it. We grew closer as friends as our senior year went on. It was time for prom. I asked him if he was going and he said, "I don't know." His girlfriend's Sweet 16 was the same weekend. He asked if I was going.

I told him, "I can't afford to go to no prom."

He said, "I'll buy your dress."

I looked at him in disbelief. "Stop playing!" I was stunned.

He did just what he said. He paid for most of my stuff to go to prom. I was hoping he was going to come so I could dance with him that night. For the first time, I didn't have a date. Yep, I went to prom as a third wheel to Val and her date.

At the time of writing this, I still own that dress. It may be time to give it up!

It was time for graduation. I was proud of myself because even though a lot of people counted me out—family, friends, and naysayers—I did it; and I did it with a nine-month-old **baby**!

All of that happened before I was legal! Year 18 of my life was calm from drama. I was coming to grips with the reality of adult life. But let me tell you, I picked up some habits. I found new ways of coping with my emotions. More sex, smoking weed, drinking, going to clubs three or more days of the week. All of that was happening while I was studying to become a medical assistant. I was doing good, trying to maintain. I completed all my classes with a B or better until my little guy took ill.

That month of school wasn't good for me. It was a month before graduation. I had one class left. I received a C for a grade in that class, so I was required to sit out for a month. I pleaded with my school because I had **ONE** class left to be a certified medical assistant. But they told me no. Once I sat out for that month, I tried to return, but the love wasn't there anymore, so I dropped out. Because I felt like a failure, I did everything that made me feel good.

By the age of 19, things started to get more adult like. I was with Kevin again and he had gotten an apartment. Things were going well with us for a little while. My son and I spent a lot of time there, so this allowed us to parent my son. We didn't always agree about situations, but I knew it was because we were raised differently. I cooked, I cleaned, I worked, I ironed his clothes for work. We paid the bills and maintained living the carefree life as if we were married. I got pregnant. Even though we were parenting my son together, I don't think Kevin was ready to be a dad.

Things started to spiral out of control between us. We argued all the time. This pushed us further apart, but I was determined to be with this man. His thought process was totally different than mine. I will never forget one day when we were home, the house phone rang. I answered and there was a female on the other end. She was about to say, "who is this," but she caught herself and she asked to speak to him. I called him to the phone. When he hung up, I asked "Who was that?" He brushed it off and said it was his supervisor. I thought no more about it.

A couple of weeks went by, and I was doing laundry. I went to put away his clothes and there was an open box of condoms in his drawer. I know we didn't use them, so I called and asked him about them. He made up some excuse, that I believed. Things didn't feel right for me, so we started arguing even more all the time, and he was always working late. He was fed up, so he put me and my baby out a couple of times. One night we got into a big argument, and it was about 9 o'clock at night. His cell phone was ringing, and he wouldn't answer it. This night he didn't work, nor did he go out with co-workers or anything like that.

I asked him why he wasn't answering the phone. The next thing I knew he decided to take the garbage out. It wasn't full, but he needed a reason to get out of the apartment. When he went to take the garbage out, I went to stand on the balcony because it faced the dumpster. Something didn't feel right. I watched him walk to the dumpster, pull out his phone and make a call. I watched him talk on his phone for several minutes. I was mad. I stepped back into the apartment and waited for him to come in. I confronted him about what I saw, and another argument broke out. He told me that I could get out.

I said, "I'm not going anywhere."

He picked my son up by one of his arms and put him out the door. I wasn't going to leave my baby out the door, so I called my mom and stepdad to come get us. I was upset and embarrassed. Here I am a mother of one and pregnant with baby number two. I couldn't believe what was happening. But I was so naive I thought that he loved me and maybe how he treated me was what love looked like. Because I didn't want to go back to my mom's house, I started living with my grandmother. I didn't go back to my mom because I didn't want to hear the "I told you so" from her about Kevin.

She used to tell me, "Anyone that loves you wouldn't hurt you or make you cry."

I didn't want to believe her because I wanted to believe he loved me. While living with my grandmother, Kevin and I stayed in communication. It was my understanding that we were going to be a family after I had our baby. I was eight months pregnant sleeping on a mattress on the floor with my three-year-old son. Kevin decided to move into a two-bedroom apartment so that we had more room for when I came back with the babies.

He was living his best life. He had a baby on the way with me and a girlfriend on the side who was older. She was giving him all the pleasures, I was not. And although, he had the two-bedroom apartment, he never once asked me to come home. I slept on the floor until the day I went to the hospital to have our baby. But I knew something was up because I would sometimes get my mom's car or my grandma's car and go sit in the parking lot of the apartment building and wait for him to come home. He never did. Sometimes I would fall asleep waiting. I never asked him about it because I knew. I just didn't want to hear it.

I felt like I was living a bad dream; and I hoped once the baby was born all things would be back to normal. In the meantime, I applied for Section 8 (subsidized housing) because I was homeless and weeks away from having two kids. I knew I needed a Plan B because I had never, by that point, spent a night in the two-bedroom apartment that Kevin had moved into. I don't remember what prompted it, but we were having a party in mid-August. We had a cookout and we had family and friends over. Kevin came to me and said, "I have co-workers coming."

I was like, "Okay, cool." It didn't matter to me because I thought that we were in a better place. I was eight months pregnant and trying to be a good girlfriend and host, showing off my hospitality skills. As I wobbled through the apartment, checking on everyone, making sure all was good, two females, supposed co-workers, came in. One of them had a gift in her hand. It was a gift for our unborn son. My mom opened the gift for me because my hands were in dish water. It was a Ralph Lauren shirt, shorts, and a hat. I thought that the gift was a nice gesture. They sat at the dining room table away from everyone else. They stayed to themselves. As the day went on, I noticed that Kevin was acting a little strange, but still trying to play it cool. My mom is an OG (original "gangsta"), and she knew the game of love, life, and relationships. So, as I hosted, she stayed close to the co-workers. Music was playing, everyone was having a great time, then Toni Braxton's song, "Just Be a Man About It," came on. I was singing as I moved around the house because I knew Kevin was seeing someone else; so, the song was fitting. One of the ladies turned to the other and said something about the song. My mom overheard them. She called me into the bedroom and asked, "Who are those girls?"

"I don't know who them hoes are, Ma. Kevin said that they're his co-workers."

"Naw, you better pay attention to that."

I started to get in tune with my surroundings and the vibe in the atmosphere. As I played the song again, I felt the shift. One of the ladies was becoming uncomfortable; she had an attitude. I then got an attitude. I started to put the pieces together. I started to say things under my breath to get a reaction from her. I called my friends and told them to come back because I thought that one of the chicks was Kevin's side chick. Yes, the side chick! The one he had been spending the nights with, the supervisor, the late work nights, the co-worker. IT WAS HER!

What nerve did he have to invite her to a party that he knew I was going to be hosting? I believe she got the hints because I made it known that I was on to her and him. She and her friend decided to leave after it became clear that being pregnant was not going to stop me from fighting. I was filled with rage. Kevin pretended to be drunk. He said he was going to go hang out with his friends when night fell. I determined that I wasn't leaving and commanded that he wasn't either. That was the first night I stayed in the new apartment. And I did it to be sure he didn't spend the night with her. I sat up most of the night, I was in disbelief. I couldn't understand why he wanted to hurt me like that. He really didn't care, but I couldn't see it, I was blinded by love.

The Section 8 I applied for was approved within three months. To my understanding that quick of an approval never happened. God has a way of making things happen for you when you don't even know that He's working. It was September and I turned 20. My baby was due in a few weeks. There were still things I needed, most importantly, transportation. So, I bought a used car. It was a burgundy Geo Metro that I paid $900 for. I got it to my grandma's house, grabbed a bucket of water and some cleaner, crawled in, with my big nine-month pregnant belly, and I shampooed the seats and floors. I needed it clean before I put my kids in there. I was nesting, preparing to be a mother of two.

I attended my last doctor's visit and because I had a C-section with the first child, Dr. Szeja already knew that I would have to have another. We scheduled to have it on my mom's birthday, September 28th. The day came, and it was time to welcome my second baby boy into the world. It felt great because I knew for sure that all my problems were about to be over because Kevin loved me—right!

Well, the first night after having the baby, he had other things to do rather than stay at the hospital with me. He came in early the next morning. The next day at the hospital, he spent most of the day in and out. He claimed that he spent that night getting the apartment ready, so I was excited. He didn't spend the next night with me at the hospital either. We came home on a Sunday. What I thought was home. Having my second C-section, I knew how to take care of myself. Things were okay for me, and I was sure that things would start to pan out and be great.

NOPE! My oldest son got sick.

I had a newborn, stitches, and staples, and a sick three-year-old. As I moved like a snail around the apartment to take care of us, things were starting to take a toll on me. I was overexerting myself. Ignoring the physical, mental, and emotional pain I was in, I would call Kevin at work to bring meds and stuff home for my three-year-old to get better. When he did, I would rave about what he had done to make him feel good about being a dad, but that didn't work. He still didn't want me.

Every morning around three thirty or so, I would call my mom crying because Kevin didn't come home. After talking to my mom, I would call him a few times. He would answer with some lame excuse about falling asleep at his homeboy's house and then come home to get ready for work.

Every day it was the same thing. He had a routine. He would come home from work for about hour, long enough to prepare for his night out; he always had some where to go. Every night when he came home, he would greet the boys, grab his clothes, and head for the shower. He always showered before he left. While in there, he would listen to this R&B singer, Sisqo's song, *Incomplete*. I thought that he was singing about me and thinking about me...lol HE WAS NOT! I HATE that song even now. It had been about two weeks since I'd come home with the baby, and this was happening EVERY NIGHT. I couldn't take it anymore. My mom drove school buses, so she would have a break during the day, and she would often visit me. That morning I didn't want a visit.

I called my mom and asked her, "When you get off your bus, can you come get me and my things."

I was hurt, fed up, and tired. I felt a pain that I could not touch, but I knew it was there. You know like when the doctor says if you can touch the pain, that's a good sign. But if you can't then seek medical attention because it's critical. That's the pain I felt.

That morning, I had gotten up early and packed my things. When my mom got there, I had all my things next to the door. I was in tears and ready to go. I remember telling her that I couldn't take it anymore. I explained that Kevin was not coming home until four or five o'clock in the morning and I couldn't take it anymore. I just wanted out. She gathered me, my kids, and my things, and we left. My mom lived in a two-bedroom townhouse. It was the ideal fit for her, my dad, and my baby brother. But once again, I was homeless and needed my mom. Me and my two babies moved in.

I questioned myself, repeatedly. Why did I keep going back? Why did I keep allowing him to crush me? This man kept breaking my heart and I kept going back like a crazy person. Was I addicted to pain or the familiarity? After I moved back with my family, the feelings of abandonment and rejection were being watered and it was tormenting my mind, daily. Somehow, I started to gain stability. I wasn't crying every day and I was starting to be the single parent that I was.

Kevin was living his best life with his new boo. He would come over talking to his girlfriend on the phone in front of me. Not one time would he ask me to come back home or how I was doing. He made it seem as if he clearly didn't care. He worked at Verizon and because of that, we had cell phone services through them. Because he got a phone for me, I thought he cared—at least a little. One day, he came over to visit and the cell he got for me mysteriously disappeared when he left. He didn't say anything, but he was pissed because I had called the "co-worker" or "supervisor" from the gathering, the one who had called our home, from my cell phone. He was heavily involved with the chick, at that point.

He took the phone so that I wouldn't have any means of communication other than my mother's landline phone service. As I think about it now, how selfish. He didn't want me to call his girlfriend or him. As I sat in my six-to-eight-week healing process, my thoughts would be all over the place. The less I cried, the angrier I became. I couldn't believe this was happening again. This man said to me he loved me. This is the same man that told me when I was sixteen and scared that he would be there for me. So how did we get here? I was confused. This wasn't enough. This was not how life was supposed to be.

# Reflection page

_____

_____

_____

_____

_____

_____

_____

_____

_____

_____

_____

_____

_____

_____

_____

_____

_____

_____

_____

# Reflection

_____

_____

_____

_____

_____

_____

_____

_____

_____

_____

_____

_____

_____

_____

_____

_____

_____

_____

# THIS ISN'T ENOUGH
## (But He kept me)

THIS ISN'T ENOUGH!!!! I Screamed at The Top of My Lungs.

Being saved and having God as my Lord and Savior was not enough for me. I didn't know how to activate anything. Man, I thought after I accepted Christ, at some point the magic would begin. Like all my problems, hurts, and disappointments would disappear. I thought that everything got better after you confessed and got baptized. I was baptized at 20. But boy, was I wrong! It seemed like things got worse.

Are you ready for this chapter? Let's begin!

The good old age of 20. In February of 2001, my apartment was ready. Brand spanking new apartment that no one had lived in! I didn't have anything, but I went with what we had—our clothes. I bought a couple of lawn chairs for my living room. I was so excited about being in my own place that I didn't care that I didn't have anything. My family got word that I was living in a bare place. Let me show you God and favor. A friend of my grandfather gave me a full bedroom set for myself. My uncle gave me a bunk bed for the boys. My brother (the one I thought hated me) gave me his entire living room set from his apartment. My mom gave me a dinette set so that we had a place to eat. My grandmother gave me towels, wash cloths, sheets, and things for the beds. Within a week those two bedrooms and two bathrooms were well stocked and furnished. Things were looking up for me. My babies were three years old and five months old, and they were my world. If they were happy, I was happy. Well, I pretended to be.

At night, I got lonely. I wanted to be someone's girlfriend so bad. My oldest son, Poppa, used to say every night before bed, "I love you, Mommy." I would tell him I loved him too, but it made me so angry when he used to say that. I would wonder why he always told me that. Didn't he know already that I loved him? When I reflect on it, I know that was God speaking through him. I didn't believe in love, but I wanted it. I didn't understand that God is love and love is God. He was three. How did he know to tell me that? I wanted love from a man, not my son. It didn't feel like or look like what I thought love was. Here I was a welfare, Section 8 mom, with no man. Typical statistic of an angry Black woman. Although I started working, I wasn't making enough, so I still qualified for benefits from the state. I did not receive any child support or anything from either father, but I was doing okay for us. We had a roof over our heads, clothes on our backs, and food on our table. We had what we needed. About three to six months into me having my own place and doing things on my own, Kevin started to come back around. He was trying to mend things between us. He was living his life with his girlfriend but making sure that I wasn't dating anyone. He started spending more time with us. One day we were having family time in the living room, and he said to me "What if I say I wanna give us another try. I will move in with you, and we work on us."

I was such a fool for him. I said, "Yes." I was excited that he wanted to be with me again, well, at least I thought. He moved in about a week or so later. I thought that he really wanted to be with me. He laid it on thick. I believed every word he said to me. He was there about two weeks before he started staying out all night again. I would call and call, he wouldn't answer. I wouldn't see him until the next day after work. I was devastated. I couldn't believe this was happening all over again. I wouldn't tell anyone because I didn't want to look like a fool. I started going through his things on the nights he wouldn't come home, and I found that he really didn't want to get back together. He was **EVICTED** from his apartment, and I guess he had nowhere to go. That's why he gave me that song and dance about living together and working on us. Time went on and he was back and forth between houses. Side chick's (same girl) and mine; funny thing was I actually may have been the side chick. I allowed this to happen because I believed that old saying "having a piece of man is better than having no man at all." I believed the lies that no one would want to date me since I was a single parent of two.

The next year rolled around, and we were still playing the same old game. This was the straw that broke the camel's back (for that moment). His birthday was in March, so he was telling me about plans to go to Orlando with his homeboys for the weekend. I thought that was a cool idea. I bought him outfits, gave him money, and told him to have fun. Yes me, the Section 8 welfare mom, with the minimum wage job.

While he was gone, I called to see if he was having a good time. But every time I called; he wouldn't answer. He named the friends that were going with him early on, so I called one of them and he answered. I asked him if they were having fun, he sounded confused by my question. He was also a mutual friend. I asked him, "Aren't you out of town with Kevin?"

He said "No."

My heart started to pound. The air started to get thick, and I couldn't breathe. My eyes welled with tears, and I hung up. My mind was racing. I started to pace the floor because I couldn't believe this was happening. My momma always told me stop looking for things because you will always find them, and your feelings will be hurt. I heard that in my head so simple, so I did just that.

I sat on the floor and started going through his things. I found a calendar/planner. I started to flip through the calendar and there it was! **MY WEEKEND GET AWAY WITH MY BABY!** It WASN'T his writing. I felt like someone had snatched my whole heart out of my chest. I started calling his phone nonstop until he answered. When he answered and I asked him what happened, he said nothing and hung up the phone. I was furious. I started packing his things so when he returned, he could get out. When he returned, he acted like it was a normal Sunday afternoon, I had his things packed and waiting for him. He was pissed off. There was a lot of arguing, some pushing and shoving, and that led to me calling my mom and stepdad to come over to put him out. I immediately changed my locks because he wouldn't give me the key back. It was a nightmare from hell. I was really done (well, I thought).

Weeks passed, and once again, he was back and forth between houses, and it was June. Some of my family members and I decided that we wanted to have a big birthday party. Our birthdays were in September. I was turning 21, SO I WAS READY! There were five of us for this party. My mom, my brother, two of my cousins, and myself. We would meet to plan and I was excited. I had something else to focus on for a little while. We all had an invite list. We decided to have the party at a night club. This night club was managed by another one of our cousins, so it was perfect. "Club Apollo" was packed. I invited everyone, guys I liked, guys that liked me, old boyfriends, all my friends, I mean everyone I thought would come. I wanted to be seen for a night, because after going through everything with Kevin, my self-esteem and self-worth were extremely low. Most of those invited came to the party. I made sure I had the cutest outfit that I could afford. I had my hair done, nails done, everything done. I was ready! Thinking about it now makes me smile because it was that party that made me the happiest then. But everything didn't go according to plan. Vallerie walked out of the party about halfway through because of a misunderstanding and that was the end of our friendship. The party was over and although it was EVERYTHING, I lost my best friend, and I didn't know why.

I called a few times the night of the party and a few times the next day, but no answer. I tried a few more times later in the week and a few times in the weeks that came, but still no answer. I was hurt, but I was used to being hurt; so, I put that where I put everything else and moved on. I had learned how to bury my feelings and everything that didn't feel good. It was hard at first, but I managed. I started preparing for my baby's first birthday. His birthday was in September as well. The time rolled around, and we had the party. Everything was good. Kevin was back, but **NOTHING** changed. He was still not coming home at night. It got to the point that when he left for work, I would go check the closet to see if he took his overnight bag when he left. If the bag was gone, I already knew he wasn't coming home. One morning I called his phone because he didn't come home, and he was not answering. I called her phone and she answered. She and I were having words and then he got on the phone and said, "Bit**, don't call her phone."

While saying this to me, I heard in the background the zipper of his overnight bag. To this day when I hear a zipper I sometimes think about that moment and cringe. I changed my locks again. He came the next morning and tried to get in and his key didn't work. He beat and beat on the door, and I wouldn't answer. The beating on the door woke the boys; they didn't know what was going on. I took the kids and went into my room. We sat on the floor in front of my bed. The next thing I knew, there were keys flying through my bedroom window. Glass shattered all over my bed. I held my babies close to me and I cried. I was hoping that he would leave. And he did. I had the apartment people come over to fix my window, but it took a few days. Because of the broken window I was afraid to leave home. We stayed home for days until the window was fixed.

By this time, we were approaching the end of 2001. I was sitting in the living room trying to figure out how I ended up with someone like that. Why was this happening to me? Why couldn't I find someone to love me for real?

Then, I had a vision. It was a vision of Kevin and I talking under a light pole. We were having a conversation about his girlfriend being pregnant. And in the daydream, it was revealed that it was a boy. When he came over, I told him about the vision. And he said that I was tripping and no, she was not pregnant. I told him that she was pregnant and that she was having a boy because if it was a girl, I wouldn't be able to handle it. Shortly after that, I found out that I was pregnant. I COULD NOT believe it. About a month went by before I told Kevin that I was pregnant. He begged me to have an abortion because of what he thought were the circumstances. I would never forget how we were standing by the refrigerator with the freezer open and he pleaded with me about having an abortion. I told him no I wasn't doing it. We were not living together; he was full time with his love.

In April 2002, my phone rang, and it was Kevin. I answered because it wasn't unusual for him to call me on his way to work. I would never forget, it was a Friday morning.

He said, "I have something to tell you." There was a long pause then a deep sigh. He uttered, "I have a baby."

I screamed, "WHAT?!"

He repeated himself. "I have a baby."

"What? When? How old is the baby?"

He replied, "A week old."

I started to scream and cry. I told him that I hated him and not to ever call me again. Why was I surprised when God had already showed me? I hung up in his face, and I cried like a baby getting its first set of shots. You know, in disbelief, but there was still pain. I wasn't sure what was happening to my heart, but it hurt. I got myself together while he called repeatedly. I finally answered and said, "I hate you, stop calling me." And I hung up the phone.

I stared at the phone while he called back-to-back. I watched it ring and with each time, I wanted to kill him.

I reached for the phone, and I called his mom at work. She answered, and she seemed a little out of it.

"I need to ask you something."

There was a pause, and I heard her crying.

I groaned, "Never mind, you already answered."

I hung up and I cried some more. By this time

Kevin was knocking on my door. I asked him to go away, and he said, "I'm not leaving until you talk to me."

I opened the front door, turned away, and walked into my bedroom, and shut the door. I sat on the edge of my bed with my head in my hands. I didn't want to talk to him. I cried and I cried because I couldn't believe that he begged me to have an abortion when he had a baby on the way the entire time. I'm glad that I didn't listen to him. That situation tore me apart. While going through all this, I was losing family members one after the other. My stress levels were high.

# MY GREATEST LOSS

I had a doctor's appointment where the doctor told me, "The baby has some abnormalities and a weak heart." I thought *you got to be kidding me*. He went on to say that he wanted to send me to a specialist. Within a week I had an appointment with the specialist, and he confirmed the things my doctor had told me. My baby would possibly have special needs with a weak heart, and immediately after birth he would have to go into open heart surgery. I was a 22-year-old single mom, with two healthy sons, and now this! My brain was on overload. Plus, they couldn't guarantee that he would survive the surgery. The doctor said, "You can go full term or it's still early enough to terminate."

"Terminate!? What does that mean?"

He said, "Abort."

It felt like he punched me in the chest and all the air had left my body. I was taking blow after blow. I was enraged sitting in that doctor's office. Anger was the only emotion that I was okay with feeling. My mom continued to talk to the doctor because I zoned out.

When we left, I told my mom that I couldn't afford an abortion. I cried, "Ma, what am I going to do with a special needs child? It's already hard with the two. Ma, what if he dies during surgery? What will I do?"

My mind was racing. I was rambling out all these questions without giving my mom a chance to answer. I had a week to let the doctor know what I decided to do. **THAT WAS ONE OF THE LONGEST WEEKS OF MY LIFE.**

I talked to my uncle, the one who walked me through salvation, and he told me that I would be okay and that I could take care of a special needs child. I couldn't see or understand how I would be able to do that. I wasn't sure. I remember thinking if **THIS** is what it's like to serve God, I can't do this. I was giving up on my faith. I talked to my aunt in North Carolina, I told her the same things and that I was leaning toward termination.

She said, "Baby, it is totally your choice."

By the end of the week, I had decided to terminate. I was a few days from six months. So, they set me up immediately with a clinic because it had to be done within 24 weeks of pregnancy. The person at the clinic asked me the necessary questions like was someone making me do this? Do I understand? There was a long list of questions. They were talking, but I wasn't really listening. You know how you could be there, but not there? That was me. My physical body was there, but my mind wasn't. It was like the person was talking to an empty shell. I didn't hear much of anything. I was in total disbelief that I was in this situation. While the lady was talking, I told them, "I have no money."

The lady said that I qualified for some program because of my circumstances. After coming out of that office and sitting in the waiting room, I was numb. I was fighting to be present. I was there, but I wasn't. It was like I was under 30 feet of water fighting to get back to the top so that I could breathe. They called my name to go to the back. That place was like a small hospital, it was ice cold with bright white walls. As I followed the nurse down the hallway and into a room, I wrapped my arms around myself. She told me to lie down on an exam table. I looked at the black bed with the paper on it and laid there for a sonogram/ultrasound.

She said, "We need to check the baby."

We listened for his heartbeat; it was faint. Then, she asked if I wanted to see it. I turned my head slightly to the right and there it was, his heart, a heart that was barely beating. She told me that she was going to give me a shot into my stomach to stop his heartbeat. I turned my head and looked at the ceiling. I laid there without a word. In my mind, I was apologizing to my unborn son. I turned back to watch the monitor and the tears started. I got the shot, and I laid there on that cold black bed for a minute getting my thoughts together. I got up, wiped the ultrasound cream off my stomach, fixed my clothes, and left. The drive home was extremely quiet. I fought the tears because I didn't want to upset my mom. I felt that I needed to be strong for her, because if she knew how much I hurt in that moment, she would have NEVER let me go through with any of it.

The night after the shot, I laid in bed, and I talked to Jahiem. I had already named him. I told him that I was sorry and that I loved him. I asked him to forgive me and that I wouldn't know how to care for him. I rubbed my stomach until his death. I don't know when his heart stopped exactly, but something in me just knew. I laid there alone, and I cried as I cuddled my dead baby in my womb. I had to return the next day to give birth. I didn't get much sleep that night. I went back to the clinic the next morning and they had a space available for me, my mom, and my grandma. The nurse explained to me what was going to happen.

The meds to induce labor began. For the first couple of hours, I didn't feel anything. I sat in the chair, looking out of the room, watching girls come in and out with no remorse. I think by hour six, the pain started. I didn't know what was happening. The nurse explained that I was having contractions. I didn't know what contractions felt like because the first pregnancy I didn't feel them. The second pregnancy was a scheduled C-section. This was new to me. There were about five of us total in this facility that had to give birth. The pain got more intense over the time.

The nurse came to me and said, "Honey, you have to start walking around."

I got up and started to walk around and there was another girl walking. We started walking together, and we talked. She shared her story with me. She was six months pregnant with a baby whose skull or brain wasn't developing, so she had to terminate. I walked around the facility for what felt like forever, up and down the cold hallways. The contractions were so unbearable, it was one of the worst pains I had ever felt. Every time I had a contraction, I would bend over and clutch my stomach. I was crying and tired. I talked with my Aunt Minnie on the phone, she prayed with me, and told me to stop holding on to guilt. She told me that I could do it.

The nurse told me to remember that Jahiem could not help me and that I must do it all on my own. She said, "When you have a contraction, you have to stay standing straight up and breathe through it."

I grabbed my CD Walkman and put in one of my favorite gospel artists, Shirley Caesar, and I started walking. I had it blasting in my ears; somehow I thought that the louder it was the more it would help with the pain. Every time that I had a contraction, I stood through it and breathed. It was work! I took breaks, but around 9pm, I was ready to go. I had been there all day. I continued to walk. I walked and walked. About 11pm, I was sitting down, taking a break and I got the urge to pee. The nurse had already told me to let her know if I had to use the restroom. On the way to the restroom, I stopped by the nurse's station. I informed her that I had to use the restroom. She said "Okay," but she didn't move.

At least I thought she didn't. I sat down to pee, and it didn't feel right.

So, I started to yell. "Hey something is happening, something is happening!"

The nurse came in. "Relax, it's going to be okay."

She put on her gloves and sat in front of me to check me while I was on the toilet. "Baby you are in labor and it's time to push."

I said, "On the toilet?!"

She smiled, and said, "Yes."

I was now freaking out. She was very calm. She checked me again. "This booger is breeched."

"What does that mean?" I asked.

"He is feet first. When I say push, I want you to push as hard as you can."

She positioned herself a little better and said, "Alright, push!"

I pushed until I was tired. She allowed me to rest for a couple of minutes.

She said, "Okay, one more push."

I gave it a good push and he was out.

"I got him," she uttered.

I turned my head as she pulled him out and placed him into this small tub. Then, she told me to push again as she pushed on my stomach. Something else came out, which I now know was the afterbirth. I sat there on the toilet, crying because my feelings were all over the place. She turned on the shower and told me to get in. I cried the entire time.

She helped me bathe, she got me out of the shower, she helped me dress, and she walked me down the hall to my room. My mom and grandmother were waiting for me. She helped me get into the bed. I lay there and I was in a space. My mom checked on me and my grandma, too. I was silent. The nurse came in and I was staring at the snow-white wall. She walked over to me, and she asked if I was okay, I didn't answer. She then asked if I wanted to see him. I told her "Yes." She had him all cleaned up. I looked at him, and he had hair already and his hand was balled up into a fist. A tear rolled down my face and I looked away. I couldn't believe that I was looking at my deceased son in a small tub. She took him away. I stared back at the wall. I wasn't talking, she asked something like, "What would I like to do with him?" or something. I wasn't listening. So, from that day to this one, I don't know what happened with his remains. That's the only regret I have. I just knew that I would have him in my heart forever. That day I felt a void. It felt like a piece of me was missing. An empty space that nothing could fill. I had to stay there at the facility for a few hours, but I was persistent about going home. I didn't want to be there anymore, I wanted to go home. It was like every emotion hit me at once and I was angry. I was not supposed to go home so quickly, but I wanted to. My mom said that she would stay with me, so they let me go home.

That night was one I won't ever forget. My mom and I were asleep in my bed. I jumped up flipping covers, moving pillows, looking around. I was looking for Jahiem because I heard him crying, I was frantic because I couldn't find him. My mom woke up and asked me, "What are you looking for?"

I look at her strangely, and I told her, "The baby, you don't hear him crying?"

She looked at me and I stopped and looked at her. On her face was confusion and sadness at the same time, and then I remembered what happened. I cried myself back to sleep. June 29, 2002 was the day I gave birth to Jahiem, and it was a day I would forever remember.

After going through that, I was still losing loved ones. I was at one of my family member's wake. One of my favorite cousins came up to me.

"Hey, Lil Terry!" I loved him SO much. I looked up to him, he was about four years older than me. I just wanted to talk to him and tell him all that I was going through. I thought that somehow telling him, that he would help me sort it all out and things would get better.

I was the baby of our bunch, so he was protective. I told him to come see me so we could talk. I told him that I was grown now, and I had my own spot, and he must come see it. He agreed. We did the funeral, and life went on. About a month later, his grandmother passed. That was extremely hard for him. We were at the wake for his grandmother, and he was taking it awfully hard. His grandmother was his everything. Not only were our fathers brothers, but our mothers are also best friends to this day. So, when we went to our granny's house, we were together, and when we were with our mothers, we were together. It was like we were related on both sides. While we were at his grandmother's wake, I went to him, and I told him that I loved him. He didn't say anything. He grabbed me and gave me a hug like never before, but he didn't say a word. It was the tightest and longest hug he had ever given me. I can feel his touch now as I type this.

A couple of weeks later my mom called me at five

o'clock in the morning. I rolled over and grabbed the cordless phone.

"Hello!" My mom sounded okay, but something was in her voice. "What you doin'?" This wasn't unusual for her to ask.

I told her I was sleeping. There was a short pause. Then she shared, "Terry is dead."

I couldn't understand what she was saying to me, "Huh?"

She repeated herself and added that he was in a car accident and that was all she knew. We hung up, I got up out the bed and walked around my room to grab my towel and some clothes. I ran a bath, and I sat in it for an hour trying to process what my mom said to me. My brain was rejecting the information that was given to me. My heart couldn't accept that he was dead. I just lost my son, there was no way that my favorite cousin could be gone, too.

I got up from the bath to shower, still in a daze. I woke the kids up and got them ready for daycare and school. The entire time, I was in disbelief. There was no way that this could have happened. I just saw him and talked to him. He was supposed to come to my house so that we could talk some more. I needed him.

I put the children in the daycare van and went

back into the house. I walked into my bedroom, grabbed the remote control off the bed, and I stood in front of my television. I turned on the news and there was the car accident story. They never said his name, but when I saw his car, all crumbled up on the news, my eyes filled with tears. Everything my mom had said came back to me and it sunk in. I lost it. I called my mom crying hysterically. My heart hurt, it felt like someone was tugging on it. I wrapped my arms around myself to calm me a little. I sat on the floor between my dresser and bed, and I cried. I was so numb. My mom and my grandmother came over; I don't remember letting them into my apartment, but I know I had to because my mom didn't have a key. I was so hurt, and I couldn't believe that God would take him away from me. Twenty-five years old and he was gone. I couldn't understand.

I knew that I had to keep going, so, I put my favorite mask on—"I'm okay!" I didn't cry anymore after that day. A few days passed and the wake rolled around. I had made up in my mind that I was going to be there for his "baby momma" and his sister because they loved him so much, and they were going to need someone to be strong for them. That was me, I was going to be the strong one. I was in that level of denial that I was going to be strong for them. They didn't want to go in and view his body. I was like, "Come on, I will go with you. It will be okay."

They trusted me, so we walked inside the funeral home. We stood at the entrance for a couple of seconds. I comforted them because I was the strong one. We walked toward the room his body was in and as soon as we turned left to enter, I saw my cousin laying in that casket and I LOST it! I was supposed to be the supporter but ended up needing support. I couldn't believe it! He was dead. I felt myself going to the ground. It was like my legs turned to jelly and they could no longer hold me up.

As I was going down, I heard my other cousin saying, "Get the baby, get the baby out of here."

All the emotions that I had bottled up and stored away under the "I'm okay" mask, burst out and I couldn't hide it. I wasn't okay! This was the second time in less than a month that I had lost someone close to me. I cried for weeks.

I was broken and I didn't want to live anymore. This thing called life was too hard. I wanted to give up on everything, especially God. I decided that I was going to believe in God, BUT I didn't want to follow Him too close. My life became a wreck. Then,

I tried to live right, but I slipped and fell and messed up. But I was trying to live this saved life because it was what I knew to be right, it just didn't work for me. My life became harder, so to fight back I again started smoking weed (marijuana) more, I was drinking more, I was going out to the clubs more, sleeping around, and I just didn't care. I had become reckless.

There was this one day I was going to smoke a blunt. I had it in my hand and my baby, Jamarcus, asked, "Mommy, what are you going to do with that?"

I looked down at him because he was three at the time and gave him a *who were you talking to* face. I replied, "Smoke it."

He looked up at me with his big eyes and in his three-year-old voice, he said, "MOMMY, GIRLS DON'T SMOKE!"

He said it with such conviction that I put that blunt down on the counter and stopped smoking, cold turkey. Life was hard and the more I fought back, it seemed like there was no change for me. Life was happening and I couldn't get a grip on it. I wanted to give up, but I had two sons that needed me, so, I kept pressing; even though it didn't seem like God was anywhere around or even cared.

I said that I would try the "God thing" one more

time. I started attending church regularly again. I watched everyone in praise and worship, and I wondered, what the laying out, crying, shouting, running, and dancing was all about. The God I served didn't make me want to do any of that. I would watch my uncle, Gene, closely. I always wanted to have my uncle's relationship with God because God was smiling on him. His life was tough, but he had this peace about him in every situation; and the way he prayed, I wanted to pray like that. But I didn't get his faith. I used to play my gospel music in my apartment and sing along, hoping to feel what I saw in church. Something in me that made me want to cry. That something that made me want to scream, dance, praise, but it didn't happen. I remember walking to the store with my boys. On the way, I decided that I was going to start talking to God aloud. I started thanking God. I didn't know how to pray anything other than The Lord's Prayer, so I just thanked Him over and over and I did it from my heart. On the way back I was doing the same and I felt something on the inside, it was hard to describe the feeling, but something that I never felt on the inside of me was coming over me. It was coupled with this warm sensation. It scared me, so I stopped telling God thank you. I stopped thinking about God. I stopped talking to Him. All I could think about was the lady in the church from when I was six years old that was shouting on the pew I was sitting on, and I thought she was having a seizure, or something was seriously wrong. I didn't want that to happen to me. But after that walking to the store encounter, I started to talk to God more, and whenever I felt that feeling, I would shut down. Something was changing in me after each encounter, but I wasn't sure what it was.

One day I was riding across the bridge on 56th Street with my momma. I spoke, "Ma, I'm tired of my life being this way. By the time I'm **40**, I need my life to be in order. I'm giving myself 17 years to get my life together."

She looked at me and said, "Okay, you can do it. You can do anything you put your mind to."

And in that moment, I started trying to figure out what I was going to do.

The minute I started figuring out a plan for my life and my boys, Jamarcus got sick, or something happened where he had to go to the doctor. The doctor listened to him, and she said, "I need you to take him to a cardiologist."

He had an abnormal heartbeat. My heart dropped;

she had to be kidding me. All the thoughts of Jahiem and his heart came to mind. I called Kevin in tears and told him that we had to take JD to a heart specialist. I explained to him what the doctor said. We had an appointment in a few days, and we took him to the specialist, who told us that our baby had a hole in his heart. I broke down. *This cannot be happening again. God, I can't lose another baby.* He was only three years old. I called my mom, Kevin's mom, and other family that I knew would pray. I was like, "Okay, God, I need to see you now." I started praying what I knew and how I knew. I cried and called out to God for Him to rescue my baby. I begged Him to not take another baby away from me. I told Him that I didn't know if I would survive one more loss. *Please God!*

We had another appointment set up for a few weeks later to discuss what we were going to do. The first doctor had suggested surgery. We went to the second appointment and that doctor said there was **no** hole in his heart. I asked if he was sure because I saw the hole myself. He turned the monitor on and there was no hole. My eyes welled up and I was filled with so much joy. I thought if God could do that, what else could He do. I started to get more interested in God. I started attending church more because I wanted to learn more about the God I served. I was trying to shift my focus because I was tired, and I wanted more out of life than what I was getting. I was stuck in a cycle that I no longer wanted to be in, but I didn't know how to get out. I felt like a hamster on a wheel, just going around and around.

By this time, I had moved from my first apartment because mold had developed in the walls, and my boys were asthmatic, so that wasn't a safe environment for them. Kevin and I moved. I had zero trust in him. Whenever he was away, I thought that he was with someone else. We continued to go through it. Things were so bad that I didn't want to live in that vicious cycle any longer. That was my first attempt at suicide. We were arguing. I walked into our bedroom because I was tired of arguing. I sat on the side of the bed. He didn't love me. *Who would miss me?* I was too scared to cut myself, so I decided to take some pills. I went to the bathroom, and there was a new bottle of Tylenol. I opened the bottle and poured a handful into my hands.

When I looked up, Kevin was standing in the doorway. "What are you doing with them?" He stared at me.

"I'm going to take them."

I started toward my mouth with them, and he ran over to knock them from my hand. Some went into my mouth and the others went flying across the room. He tried to get the ones out my mouth, but I was swallowing them one by one. We tussled for a while until he realized that they were all swallowed. He didn't know what to do but I was sure that I had taken enough to die. I felt and heard my heart beating at a rapid pace. It was like I had been running a race. Then, it started to beat slowly, so slow that I thought it would be all over in a second. I closed my eyes hoping that it was over. I didn't want to feel the pain of life anymore. Clearly, that attempt didn't work.

When the lease was up there, my Section 8 wasn't going to be renewed; I needed a plan, I didn't know what to do. My granddad was living alone in his house, and the house had an apartment on the side of it. He had been living on the apartment side because the house was too much for just him. The kids and I moved into the house. By then, I was 24 years old and trying to draw closer to God. Kevin and I were still back and forth having difficulties. For over a year I tried dating, but none of it was working for me. It was more hurt feelings after hurt feelings. During all the turmoil, I got pregnant. I couldn't believe it. I took five store pregnancy tests before I went to the doctor. PREGNANT! I couldn't be. I mean it had been four years of no birth control and I didn't get pregnant.

I had so much going through my brain. I was working and doing okay for myself, so I had a little money saved up. I decided that I was going to have an abortion. I called and made the appointment and that was going to be it. Then, I got this pain in my heart. There was this fear like never before. I was angry but scared at the same time. I didn't know what to do. The day of the appointment, I sat in the car undecided and crying. I knew it was going to be another boy and I had two with me and one in heaven. I was good. But there was something that wouldn't allow me to drive to that clinic, and today I thank God I didn't. But there I was pregnant and alone.

That was a pivotal place for me. It's where I learned how to spend time with God. I started reading more. I read this book called *The Unseen Essential: A Story for Our Troubled Times,* by James P. Gills, M.D. Then, I read another book by Stormie Omartian called *The Power of a Praying Woman.* The books rocked my world. They also gave me tools. I felt like I was getting my life in order, even though I couldn't see right from left. After those two books and all the praise and worship I was doing, I started to feel different about life. Don't get me wrong, things were still happening, but I felt different. I tried to stay positive because I didn't want to cause stress to this baby like I did Jaheim. It was just me and my boys, and life was good. I would read something every night. I started asking God what I should read. I felt like He would lead me to whatever I needed. And every time it was another nugget in my pocket. Time went on and it was time to see what the gender of the baby was. I was not excited because I was certain of the gender. I prayed and prayed for a girl, but I wasn't convinced because I prayed with Jamarcus too. I got to the hospital, and I didn't want anyone to go with me. I arrived and went in for the ultrasound. I watched the monitor for a while then I turned my head to stare at the wall with a million thoughts going through my head.

She asked, "Do you want to know the gender?"

I said, "I know it's a boy, but yes, go ahead." I turned and looked at her.

She smiled and said, "IT'S A GIRL!!!"

I was overjoyed. I asked, "Are you sure?"

She said, "Yes," and she proceeded to show me how she knew. I smiled so BIG; I showed all my teeth. I was so anxious to leave so I could tell everyone. On the way home, I stopped at Burger King to get something to eat and went to my grandma's house. She was in the kitchen cooking. I said, "Hi Grandma." I sat at the table and started to eat.

She said, "What's wrong? What did they say?"

"They said (with the biggest smile) IT'S A GIRL!"

She was so happy for me because she knew how much I wanted a girl. I couldn't wait to tell everyone.

That pregnancy was pretty smooth. The only thing she didn't like were ultrasound days. Whenever we had to get an ultrasound, she would give the technician the hardest time. She would always turn her back to them and she wouldn't allow them to get measurements. It would take forever! I was eight months and we had made it through. Well, at least I thought so. I was driving down the street, passing a gas station. There was this car coming up to the exit of the gas station, but the guys were looking one way. I thought that I could make it pass them since I was passing the exit as they were approaching it. To my surprise, I was wrong. They hit the back end of my car and kept going. I pulled over into the parking lot to see the damage to the car and there was a pain in my stomach. I clutched my stomach and started crying. I got back in the car and attempted to drive, but I was in so much pain.

I called my mom and told her what happened, and she told me to call the ambulance. I was rushed to the emergency room where the doctor said that I was having Braxton Hicks contractions. I was observed for a couple of hours and sent home. I was a few weeks from nine months, so they didn't seem worried. About a week went by and things didn't feel the same. Her movements were limited. I was so afraid.

One day she didn't move at all. With tears in my eyes, I called the doctor. The nurse told me to come in. It was January 3, 2006. My mom picked me up and we drove to the doctor's office. The car ride was quiet. I went into the doctor's office, and we went directly into the ultrasound room. She, of course, had her back turned. But no matter how they shined the light, she wouldn't move.

"Okay, we are going to shock her. It won't hurt her or you, but it will get her to move," the nurse tried to assure me.

They shocked her. Nothing. My heart dropped. I tried to understand what was happening and told myself this wasn't a repeat. "Why isn't she moving?" I asked.

She said, "Okay, we are going to shock her again." They shocked her again, she barely moved. The doctor told me that I needed to go home, get my bags, and go to the hospital immediately. I was so scared. My mom took me home and we got my bags and went to the hospital. I was admitted. I was hooked up to the baby monitor. The minute that I heard my baby's heart beat I felt relieved.

They said, "We are going to take her today." She wasn't due until the 10th of January. They acknowledged that but advised that she must come out much sooner. Some things transpired at the hospital and the operating room wasn't ready, so they changed the date to January 4th.

January 4th at five o'clock in the morning. They came in and let me know that they were going to get me ready for surgery. I was still hooked to the monitor so they could track her heartbeat. The nurse thought that she was going to be a six plus pounds baby. SHE WAS NOT! She was five pounds seven ounces. When they took her out, she cried at the top of her little lungs. They brought her over to me as she was crying.

I said to her, "Tanaejah, stop that crying, no one wants to hear that." She stopped crying and turned her head to me. They were so surprised. I told them that I have been calling her by name since I found out that she was a girl. I would have conversations with her. She was the sweetest baby.

When she was two weeks old, I noticed that she had blood in her stool. I called her doctor and took her in. She sent her to a Gastroenterologist. The specialist had her immediately admitted to St. Joseph's Children's Hospital. *My baby is only two weeks old, and she is being admitted to the hospital. Lord, why?* They picked and they probed. She cried and so did I. I was there alone. Mom and Grandma had the boys. We were there for three or four days. I was there every second. I DID NOT leave that hospital for any reason. I didn't shower until Day Two. My mom brought my clothes to the hospital. I was afraid. I didn't know what was going on; too much was happening. She was so tiny and going through so much. For a minute I thought I was being punished for giving up on Jaheim. Then, I thought I was being punished for wanting to abort her. All I thought was, *Lord please don't take my baby away from me.* We found that she had an allergy to milk. They changed her to a potato-based milk and sent us home. I was grateful.

I was still living in my grandfather's house. When she was six weeks old, I went back to work. She went to daycare. She got sick again. She didn't have to go to the hospital, but she was sick. My granddad told me to take time off work to take care of her. I was off for several months to ensure that she was okay. I thought because she was on a different milk that she wasn't getting everything that she needed. I needed to care for her myself to make sure. She continued to drink that milk until she was about 18 months. This girl was different. She was definitely different from the boys. By nine months she was starting to talk, and at 11 months, she was walking. She was always determined to do things. At about a year old, things with her took a bit of a turn.

I don't know why, but she started to be different. I started to notice that she didn't like change. As things changed around her, she would have a fit. She would scream and cry, loudly. It used to be so loud that everyone in the house, no matter where we were, would come to see what was going on. This girl made me extremely mad, often. She would get a "pow pow" with my two fingers, but for her it was enough. She would throw herself to the floor. I mean, it was bad. I thought that she was demon-possessed. There was no controlling her. I had to let her have a fit until she was done. I remembered one day it was so bad that I sat in the chair, watching helplessly. I saw myself hurting her, beating her, that's how angry I was. I didn't touch her, I just got up from the chair and walked away, crying. I couldn't contain my tears. I called my mom, and she thought that I was overwhelmed and tired. I assured her there was something wrong with Tanaejah. Once we calmed down, I went to my grandma's house. I was talking to them about what was going on. They didn't quite believe me. I was a single parent with three kids, so they all just thought I was overwhelmed. I could tell that they had sympathy for me though. I was going through a lot, even outside of the children.

One day we were getting ready to go to church and I went over to Mom's before church. I had already dressed Nae, my nickname for her. Well, we got there, Mom had a dress that she wanted her to wear. She wanted me to change her. I told her that I wasn't going to change her, and she could if she wanted to. But I told her to be aware that she was going to have one of those fits. So, she called her over and took her dress off. Mom tried to put that other dress on her and there it was—a full-blown fit. Momma could not control her. I just sat there with tears in my eyes.

Mom looked at me. "What is wrong with her?"

"I told you."

She threw herself on the floor, screaming and crying. Through my tears I could see her, and it didn't look like my baby. I told Mom, "You have to change her back. If you change her back, she will be okay."

Through the squirming fight she was doing, Momma was able to take the dress off. Once she took it off, she started to calm herself a bit. When she saw Mom with the other dress, she went over to her to put it back on. Once the first dress was back on, she was fine like nothing happened. My mom was done! She could not believe what had just happened. Then she agreed with me that I needed to make a doctor's appointment to explain what was going on with her.

We went to the doctor, and I told her what was happening. I was heartbroken because I believed something was wrong. The doctor said there was nothing wrong with her without testing her or recommending a specialist or anything. I was mad because she thought that I was trying to get a disability check or some sort for her. I wasn't. I told the doctor I was employed, and my children had Medicaid, but I was not trying to get further assistance for her. My baby truly needed help. I did my own research and took all the classes I could to figure out what was wrong and how to deal with it. My daughter taught me how to care for children that had that underlying thing that everyone ignored. I was working with children at the time, but I wanted to know more.

At age 26, I **started** college. It's never too late to make a change. I would work all day and go to school at Hillsborough Community College at night. The classes were great, but the pace was too slow for me. I stayed there until I heard about another option. It was a private college, but the pace was faster. Going there I had to make sacrifices. My boys were playing sports. This meant I missed games, lots of them. I went to school all day on the weekends. So not only did I miss my kids on the weekends and their activities, but I also missed church. As a babe in Christ, I didn't think that was a good idea. This was twice a month most semesters and sometimes every weekend depending on what class I was in. The boys would be with Kevin and Momma. Grandma would have Nae. This went on for about two and a half years. I DID IT! I graduated college with honors. I was so proud of myself. Because when I thought back, I remembered that my assistant principal from high school said that I wouldn't graduate from high school and, look at me, I became a college graduate.

During my time in college, life was not a walk in the park. Life took more twists and turns. I was trying to draw closer to God the best way I knew how. I was looking for love. I JUST WANTED TO BE LOVED! I was still reading at night before bed, so one night I decided to ask God what I should read. I felt in my spirit that He was leading me to the book of Job. I inquired, "What chapter and verse?" He told me to read the whole thing. That was the longest book ever! It took me weeks to read it. I learned so much. There are things that I hold on to today that I learned when I read the book of Job. Some of the things that were happening and had happened to me in my life started to make sense.

God knew the plan that He had for me. I had been single and celibate for about 11 months. I was doing well, but lonely as ever. I mean, I had friends, but nothing serious, just someone to talk to. I was trying to get the attention of my childhood crush. I mean, we would talk every now and then, but I wanted more. I wanted to be his girlfriend. I was so crazy about this guy. I would see him, and my heart would skip a beat. I would get extremely nervous around him. When he smiled, my heart would melt. I was head over heels in love. The first time he told me he loved me I thought that my heart was going to leave my chest. He told me he loved me! In disbelief, I called my friend, Rahneia, and screamed what he said through the phone.

He would visit me, and I would visit him, and we talked regularly. No sex, no spending the night, no dates; just conversation and enjoying one another's company. He ended up going to jail. I was so upset because I thought I was going to be his girlfriend. We stayed connected while he was gone. He would call and we would write letters, but it wasn't enough. There I was again, wanting to be in a relationship and be loved.

I was at work when one of the male parents walked in during nap time. I knew him because we went to school together. When he came in, his twin brother came in behind him. I spoke to them both but gave his brother a hug because it had been forever since I had seen him. We talked a little to catch up and exchanged numbers.

He called that night. I was surprised. We had a good conversation. The phone calls got frequent, and the conversations got better. He asked me out, so we started dating. I LIKED HIM. He spoke my love language. We got along great. Things finally were good.

I was still writing my childhood crush because there was no way that I would turn my back on him while he was locked up. My new boyfriend invited me over to his place. I went over and we chilled. Things started to get heated, so I left. I wasn't ready for any of that. He understood. I didn't think that he would still want to talk to me, but he did. I thought *this guy likes me*. We would go on dates, spend time together, he would help me cook and clean my house. He would buy me things. It felt so unreal. He started talking about marriage. That meant I had to tell Kevin that I was dating someone, and it was serious.

I called Kevin. He and the boys were at a picnic at the park for the football team. He was rude to me, as usual. "I just called because I need to tell you something."

He asked, "What, Shay?"

"I just wanted you to know that I am dating some-one, and I like him. We are going on dates, and I didn't want anyone else to tell you that they saw me out with him. It's someone we went to high school with."

I told him who it was, and he was quiet. I told him, "I am only telling you because it's getting serious."

He was speechless.

He just said, "Okay, Shay" with a shocked, but

disappointed voice. I hung up and started to breathe again. I was SO nervous to tell him because I had never told him that I was putting anyone before him.

My new boyfriend and I were perfect together. Even when we didn't agree. We listened to one another and talked it out like two adults. I WAS IN LOVE! It was happening. We started marriage counseling with my pastor. We were not living together or anything, but we spent lots and lots of time together. UNTIL…one day I was at work and my phone rang. I answered. It was him, my boyfriend.

I answered, "Hello," and there was no one, there was just noise in the background. I assumed he pocket dialed me. There was a second time my phone rang, and the same thing occurred, noise in the background. I called him to tell him that he kept pocket dialing me. There was no answer. I thought that was strange. A third time my phone rang. It was him again. This time I excused myself and went into the bathroom so I could hear more clearly what was going on in the background.

I heard him arguing with a woman. Not only was he arguing with a woman, not just any woman, but his WIFE! Yep, I said it. His wife. I WAS CRUSHED! I left work because I was angry. I wanted to go fight him. I went to my grandma's house, and I explained what happened. I went into her bathroom and I cried. I cried like a baby. I couldn't understand why he would talk to me about marriage if he already had a wife. He was calling and calling. I wouldn't answer. I had nothing to say. The next day he called. I answered. He apologized, he told me that they were separated, and he wanted a divorce. He told me that he wanted to be with me, and I didn't want to hear any of it. But I listened. I didn't take him back. He would text me every now and then to check on me, but it was nothing. I was single again.

****

My bathroom in my house was a mess and it needed some repairs. I didn't want to live with my kids in that condition so I started trying to figure out who I could live with. My granddad said that it would only take a couple of weeks to repair. I asked Kevin if we could come and stay with him for a couple of weeks. He said, "Yes. Is your boyfriend going to be okay with that?"

I said, "It's over. He is married."

We moved in with Kevin. This was 2009. Things were a bit strange because, for the first time, we weren't a couple, but we were living together. I was really hoping that the bathroom repairs would only take two weeks. Well, two weeks turned into a month. I was getting frustrated, but at the same time growing closer to Kevin. Six weeks into waiting on the bathroom to be prepared, Kevin asked if I would like to give it another try. I was hesitant, but I said, "Yes."

He said, "If we get back together this time, we are getting married."

*Yeah, right!* We were back together, and he was telling people that we were getting married. I was like, oh crap, I need to plan a wedding. So, I started making plans.

One Sunday I got up to go to church and I noticed a missed call on my cell phone. On my way to church I called the number back. No answer. I went on to church with no thoughts of it. Church was good that day. I was in a great mood afterwards. On the way back I had to pass by my granddad's house to get some clothes. I had not moved back in yet because the bathroom was still under repair. That was about month three of a two-week job. I stopped by the gas station to get gas. While the gas was pumping, I decided to text the number to see who called me earlier that morning. And it was him.

My childhood crush. I was so happy. Then, I remembered that I had just told Kevin we could try again. I didn't have a ring or an official proposal, but it was happening.

My crush and I didn't stop talking from that day. We continued to talk and text and see one another every now and then. I didn't want to lose him again. I was being selfish. This went on for months. I could tell that he was getting closer to me and that my being his girlfriend was close to happening. But I knew that I had to tell him that I was getting married. I wasn't going to drag him on because I didn't want to hurt him.

One day we were on the phone, and I knew that I had to tell him because I felt the closeness and I loved it. I took a deep breath and said, "What would you say if I told you that I was getting married?"

He said, "Congratulations."

"Thank you."

There was this long pause of dead silence. Then, he hung up. I called back. No answer. My eyes filled with tears, but I knew it was the best thing to do because I didn't want to hurt him. But I did anyway. I called back after work, and he answered. I asked, "Why you hung up?"

"Because there is nothing left to say."

"I'm sorry."

He hung up.

I haven't spoken to him since that day. I always wanted to know his thoughts and be able to answer any questions he may have had, but we never got a chance to talk.

That was over and it was wedding planning time. I would think about him often at first then I eventually stopped. Planning a wedding and thinking about my future was a lot. The bathroom still wasn't ready, so we decided to move into a bigger place. I told my granddad that I was moving, and he had a fit because, even though I wasn't there, I was still paying him rent for the house. When I realized that we were getting married for real, I told him that the money I owed him, I would make in payments. How did I owe him? I didn't work when Nae was sick and he told me to stay home with her. Well, he didn't eliminate the bills, he simply extended when I could pay them. So, I was making extra payments to him to reduce what I owed. Not one time did he ever have to remind me to pay my bills.

When I told him that I was moving out, he had a fit! He called me while I was at work and talked to me like a stranger in the street. He threatened to sue me and take me to small claims court if I didn't pay him his money in full. He was so mean and nasty to me. I owed him a balance of $622.00 from a debt of over two thousand dollars. I cried like I had lost a loved one. I did. I lost my granddad. That day he broke my heart.

Every man that was supposed to love me and protect me had hurt me. I knew that I needed to, but within my heart, I couldn't forgive him. We would never be the same. I respected him for who he was, but I felt no emotions when it came to him. I didn't want to see anything bad happen to him and I wished no harm toward him, but I just didn't have anything when it came to him. This was hard for me because we were a close-knit family. Before I moved out, I got a cashier's check and made sure that I gave it to him. We moved out and Kevin moved out of his apartment, and we found a house to rent in Temple Terrace. We moved into this house in March of 2010. I felt like my life was falling apart and coming together at the same time. We moved in, and I was planning a wedding and was completely overwhelmed.

During all that was going on, I found out that my aunt, who was one of my bridesmaids, was battling breast cancer. My God! I took that extremely hard. I was as supportive of her as I could be while considering floral arrangements, dresses, and everything else. Finally, it was the end of May, and the real countdown was on. I was having second thoughts, but I ignored them because how could God not ordain marriage. After marriage everything would be better, and things would magically change. I was on my Jesus-fix-it pill again. I still hadn't learned that's not how it goes.

I was counting down to June first. I was feeling all the emotions of what was happening. The fourth was the day of the wedding rehearsal. I spoke to God all day because I WAS STRESSED! That night we all showed up at the church. Some on time, some late. It was my wedding and I wanted everything perfect. From the music to the steps, everything! I was getting a little frustrated because some things weren't going as planned. I asked Kevin something and he snapped at me in front of everyone. We exchanged words and I stormed out of the church. Vallerie came behind me trying to calm me down. Yep! After all those years of not talking, I still asked her to be my maid of honor because I couldn't see anyone else in that place. I finally stopped across the street with tears in my eyes. "That's it! I'm done."

She looked shocked. "You have come too far. THE WEDDING IS TOMORROW!"

"I know, but if I don't get out of the limo tomorrow, know that I decided to not go through with it."

We talked and I cried. I looked at her and asked, "Am I making a mistake?"

"This is what you've been wanting for years and now it's here. You are just emotional from everything that is going on."

That night the bridesmaids and I went back to the hotel where we were staying for the night. I called Vallerie in my room and told her that I didn't want to do it. She calmed me and told me to sleep on it. None of the other bridesmaids knew what was going on, they just knew that I was upset. The next morning, I was up early staring at the ceiling. I told God I hoped that I was doing the right thing. I was twenty-nine with three kids. I wanted to be married, although there were things in me which told me not to. My heart was telling me that everything would be okay. Thinking back now, we did not have the proper marriage counseling. We had five sessions, and I didn't have any nuggets to look back on, carry me through, or hold me together.

****

It was Wedding Day! The wedding was at four o'clock in the evening. I started doing all the running around I needed to do. I was my own wedding coordinator. After getting everything together, I went back to the hotel to shower, rest, and get dressed. It was time to get ready! The videographer was late. I was mad. How could he be late? It was my wedding day. After I was dressed, he showed up. We were able to take some photos and shoot some video footage.

Something old, something new, something borrowed, something blue. I gave Vallerie a ring many years prior to the wedding and she still had it. I mean, this ring was from high school.

She opened the box and said, "I want you to have this." And there it was, the sterling ring with a blue stone. I smiled and placed it on my hand.

We took more pictures in the hotel lobby. We got into the limo. I was still in my feelings, but I was trying to be happy. On the way to the church, I looked at all the ladies and said, "If I don't get out and tell the limo driver to go, just know that I thought about it and I decided not to go through with it."

As the ladies exited the limo, they were nervous because they knew that I was serious. They all went into the church lobby, and I sat in the limo contemplating. But all the while not wanting Kevin to see me because it was bad luck, right? I saw Kevin walk up the side of the church waiting to go in. I stared at him. A tear rolled down my cheek. He went in, I took a deep breath and said, "Okay, let's do this."

Everything was perfect. The time was 3:59 and 59 seconds. We started ON time, just like we rehearsed. The steps of the wedding party were perfect. Everyone was inside and it was time for me to get out of the car. I took a deep breath and got out. I walked up to the door and took another deep breath. I stood in the lobby until it was my time. Then, BOOM! Just like that it was time for me to make my grand entrance. The doors opened, and there I was standing there in my beautiful gown, ready to enter the church. Everyone stood to their feet. My song started to play, and I began my journey down the aisle. I started walking by myself as a tribute to my dad because deep down inside I wished that he were there. I walked about one-third of the aisle before my stepdad came to meet me. He grabbed my hand and turned me around. That was something I wanted to do to represent turning a new leaf. Out with the old and in with the new. My stepdad walked me down the aisle the rest of the way. As I looked at people, the smiles, the tears, the laughter, I knew that everything was going to be all right on that day. It was PERFECT! There were a few things I didn't care for, but it all went over smoothly. THERE! The wedding was over and on to the reception. The reception was held at the West Tampa Convention Center.

The reception was everything it was supposed to be. It was time to go, and I remembered we packed all the gifts we received into the car with barely enough room for us. You know the wedding couple doesn't really get to eat at the reception, so we were hungry. We decided to stop by Wendy's. LOL! Yes, Wendy's was on the way to our hotel. We went through the drive thru. We pulled up to the window; I was still in my wedding gown, and he was still in his tuxedo. The girl at the window was surprised to see us. She started to call everyone to the window. Everyone wanted a peek, then the questions started. We simply wanted to get our food and go—which we finally did!

Once we arrived at the hotel, we looked at one another and wondered what we were supposed to do with all the stuff in the car. Yep, we left it. That next morning, we woke up as husband and wife and I was sure the magic happened overnight. I knew that God knew how bad I wanted this to be the best marriage ever. We didn't have money for a honeymoon, and I didn't mind because material things didn't excite me. We went home to unload the car. We dropped everything in the living room and went to breakfast. I was so excited to be a wife. I wanted to serve my husband and wanted my husband to serve me.

I thought that marriage was the answer to all the problems in the world because once I got married everything would magically be all right. All my wounds would heal, my past wouldn't matter, and all the hurt would diminish. Much to my surprise, I was wrong. It was the total opposite. I prayed the first year of my marriage like I had never prayed before. I learned some valuable lessons that first year. I learned that marriage was not a magic pill and marital relationships take work. I thought that love would make everything complete. Because love is all you need, right? The Bible said that love was the fix all, right? Well, at least that's what I thought it was saying. That year I learned how to pray harder, breathe deeper, and love more.

# Reflection page

## What situations can you recall where God kept you?

_____

_____

_____

_____

_____

_____

_____

_____

_____

_____

_____

_____

_____

_____

_____

_____

_____

# Reflection

_____

_____

_____

_____

_____

_____

_____

_____

_____

_____

_____

_____

_____

_____

_____

_____

_____

_____

# FORGIVENESS
## *(Unmasking)*

After getting married, things were different for me. I started praying more, I started to look at myself more and the broken pieces of me. I didn't like me. I started to seek help. I attended marriage classes, went to counseling to try and get an understanding of what marriage was. I did this because I wanted and needed my marriage to work. I didn't learn much of anything at all in the pre-marital sessions. I was on a mission because I knew that love and marriage had to be more than what I was experiencing. I was going to church every Sunday and trying to be in Bible study on Wednesdays. I just knew that if I gave God more time that he would fix my marriage and hear all my cries about me and how much I needed Him.

I prayed and cried out all the time from what I thought was my soul. I was hurting and I wasn't sure God heard me or knew that I needed Him. One

Sunday, there was an altar call for forgiveness. I went to the altar because I needed to forgive some people and just maybe things would feel lighter, and I would be able to move forward. I went up there and I prayed with one of the ladies in my church. I prayed, but I wasn't sure how to open my heart completely. I wasn't sure how to get into that place of hurt and release it. But I tried. After service, the lady I was praying with called me over and told me that she wanted to do an exercise with me. I was open to it. "Okay."

She was encouraging. "I sent my husband to the store for some balloons, and when he returns, we can get into it."

She and I had a bit of small talk, then he walked in with three balloons. The three balloons represented the people whom I prayed to forgive earlier in church service. She gave me the balloons and told me to walk around the church holding the balloons. I did as asked, and as I walked as I walked, there were people still inside the sanctuary. When I walked by them, they had to duck or dodge the balloons. When I got back to her, she asked if I saw how the people had to move around me with the balloons.

"Yes."

"That's how it is when you walk into church. The

balloons aren't there physically, but people have to maneuver around you because the weight that you carry is so heavy. We are going to pray once more over the people, and when we go outside, you are going to release the burden of unforgiveness for that person."

I started to cry because as much as I wanted to be free, I still wanted to hold on to the anger. There was one balloon for my husband, one balloon for my dad, and I'm not sure who the other one was for, but I believe my granddad. We prayed and went outside.

She comforted me with her words, "Whenever you're ready to let go, let go."

The first one I let go without a problem. The next one, I was ready to let go. It was the one that represented my dad. I was over 30, and as much as I hurt and missed my dad, it was time to let go. We would never have that father-daughter relationship that I longed for. It hurt and I cried, but it was time to let go. As the balloon left my hand, the tears rolled down my cheeks. I couldn't believe that I had to let go of my daddy.

I was down to the last balloon. She looked at me intently. "Okay, this balloon represents your husband." I looked up at the balloon and the tears were streaming down my face. I allowed myself to cry but held my composure at the same time. She said, "Whenever you are ready."

I held on to the string so tight. I didn't want to let go without an apology. I didn't want to forgive him because he hurt me profoundly. I didn't want to forget what he had done to me. I wanted to forgive but also hold on to the hurt. I thought it would all feel better once we said, "I do." But it didn't. I twirled the string and cried. I started to release the string inch by inch. I looked up at the balloon and it was getting further and further away from me. It felt okay because I still had it by the string. I was still in control. When I was ready, I LET GO. I watched that balloon until I couldn't see it anymore. I broke down in tears, no longer trying to keep my composure.

She hugged me and let me cry it out. When I finally left church that Sunday, I felt lighter but exhausted. I continued to go to church trying to remain that way - lighter. I was doing good. A couple of Sundays later we were having praise and worship. During that time, it was like this spirit of laughter came over me. But it was a different laugh. It wasn't a laugh like something was funny it was a laughter of cleansing. I laughed and I laughed. When I came out of it, it felt amazing. My mom and I talked about it later and she asked me what I was laughing at. I told her, "I don't know. It was like I wasn't there. Why? Did it sound weird?" I asked confused.

"No, it sounded like a baby laughing for the first time."

I thought that was an interesting way to describe it. I felt so good. Things were happening for me at church, so I wanted to keep going. It didn't feel like an obligation. I felt my relationship in Christ was developing more. I was good. Trying to be who I had the capacity of being, which I thought was the best version of me. In all of that, there was still one thing missing. I wanted to speak in tongues, the ability to pray in a heavenly language. I used to be asleep and hear myself praying in tongues. But when I was awake, I could never pray that way. Whenever someone would pray that way, I always felt like my spirit understood them.

It was now March of 2011. I had been growing and learning more. I was like a sponge trying to soak it all in. I was in church every Sunday. On one Sunday in March, we had another altar call for something. But I didn't go up there that time because I didn't want people to think, *man, she is needy*. And I was. I was jacked all the way up, but I didn't want anyone to know it. I didn't want to be judged. Back then, that mattered to me. I didn't know that people don't have a heaven or a hell to put me in. While everyone was up there praying, I was praying in my seat. When I looked up, my same Christ mentor who enlightened me about forgiveness was looking at me. She called me to the altar, and we prayed. Afterwards, I went back to my seat and continued to pray. I looked up again and someone else was calling me to the altar. We prayed, and then I went to sit back down again. Don't get me wrong, they were very valid prayers. This service was all praise and worship. It wasn't planned that way but that was the service we were in. I continued to pray; and, you know how you could feel someone looking at you. Yeah, that feeling. I looked up and my mentor was staring at me. I dropped my head and lifted it again; then, she motioned with her finger for me to come to her.

All I could think was, *Okay God, I have been to this altar two times already.*

She stated, "There is something that you've been asking God for and He's going to give it to you today."

I stared at her.

"You've been asking God for the gift of tongues and today is the day you're going to get it." She started to pray with me and for me. She laid her hands on my stomach and prayed. Then, she uttered, "Speak. Speak what you hear."

I heard the tongues in my spirit, but I couldn't get it out. She rubbed my neck where my vocal cords were. As she went in the upward motion, she repeated, "Speak. Speak what you hear."

And the words spilled out. I was speaking in tongues. I fell to the floor in tears, grateful that God had gifted me one more time. She prayed over my ears and told me to be careful of what I let in my ear gates.

She spoke boldly. "When you speak in your heavenly language, it may not sound like anyone else's tongues, but that is okay because it is yours and it is not supposed to." She told me that it was a new language, and I must use it to develop it. I tried it multiple times, but it didn't sound right to me, so I didn't use it often.

I carried on with life. This experience was going so well. The ability to speak in tongues for me meant my relationship with God was still developing. I was becoming more confident in who I was and whose I was. I stopped wearing the "I'm okay" mask all the time. I was developing.

There was something about the month of March for me that I hadn't quite figured out yet, but years later I had to get a partial hysterectomy. While lying in the bed, recovering from surgery, I spoke to God about some things. We talked about forgiveness. He gave me a vision of myself and the people that I was holding onto. In the vision, I was walking through life with the spirits of hurt and disappointment; and the people who hurt and disappointed me walked beside me. For example, at two-years-old my dad left, and the spirits of hurt and abandonment from him leaving walked behind me. In the vision, the line was so long; it was like a line waiting to get into a Fred Hammond or Beyoncé concert.

I saw the faces of people. People that I was holding onto that I forgot even hurt me. God showed me the weight and baggage that was keeping me bound. That was too much, so I talked to God about how I wanted to be loved, and He showed me there was a lot about me to love. That blew my mind. But I knew that I had to deal with the rest of my forgiveness issues first. I thought that I forgave half of those people, but forgiveness is a process. It's like taking up your cross every day and walking with God. You must constantly speak to your spirit man. Tell yourself that you forgive every day until it sticks, release those people. Do it until you feel the burden of the weight getting lighter and lighter. I know you were probably told to put it on the altar and leave it there. If that works for you, cool. I am not doubting the altar, but there are things that I put on the altar, and by the time I am back to my seat the same thing was waiting on me. Because my mind put it there but not my heart. Honestly, I had been through several healing exercises to help me become whole. But if you are not ready, a part of you will still hold on to the hurt. Not because you want to but, because if you clean yourself out, you will really be free and vulnerable. We would then become afraid that someone else would be able to hurt us. It was easier to keep it and just build walls to keep those in and new ones out. It just appeared to me that wall-building was fear, not protection.

We say we trust God, but do we? God does not give us the spirit of fear and because we don't want to admit it is fear, we call it protection. God equipped us with everything we need. God will give us wisdom in every area of our life if we ask. He gives us discernment, but we don't use it.

So, when we find ourselves in tough situations, we revert to God with, "Lord, you didn't see that coming? Why didn't you save me?"

I can imagine God saying, "My child, you didn't see that coming? Why didn't you use your wisdom and discernment that I have gifted you with?"

We are quick to blame God and the enemy for things that were happening or have happened in our lives, but do we not live our very own lives. I know some are saying you completely surrendered to God. I get it. But, in your surrender, God gives you something for each thing you give Him. He equips us with certain things to continue to go on. Faith, wisdom, knowledge, understanding, and discernment just to name a few.

It wasn't until this moment that I realized that I've been going through this forgiveness thing wrong. I partially forgave people so I could hold on just enough to build a wall. Or justify why I needed one. The heavier you are, the heavier your cross. And when your cross is too heavy, you no longer want to pick it up and go. Then, we start to lose the tools that God equips us with. I understood faith without works was dead. Having faith to forgive was one thing but working to forgive was a whole other ballpark. Forgiveness takes work, work we may not want to put in because it seems to be too much.

# Reflection page

Who do you need to forgive? Start with yourself.

I forgive me for…

_____

_____

_____

_____

_____

_____

_____

_____

_____

_____

_____

_____

_____

_____

# Reflection page

Who do you still need to forgive?

_____

_____

_____

_____

_____

_____

_____

_____

_____

_____

_____

_____

_____

_____

_____

_____

# IT'S UGLY!

*In this chapter, let's talk about when things got real.*

T here were so many things going on in my life that I wanted to walk away from it all. I was at that ugly stage in life where you rethink decisions that you made and wish to correct them. There was one part of my life where I sometimes allowed the devil to use me. I fell into his trap. It was the simple things around me the devil used to take me off course.

As I fought to stay in tune with Jesus, the more the devil threw blows. The area in my life that needed the most work was my marriage. Honestly, sometimes I wanted to be married and sometimes I didn't. I felt that I didn't have the energy to fight for it. I tried to understand it, but I couldn't. It escaped me the reason I was married and to whom I was married. I questioned my ability to be a wife. I knew that God had a plan, and I knew that it was all for me to go through, but I also knew that this battle was not for me, it was to help someone. And whoever I could help, I would be sure to give God all the glory and praise.

It was like we just couldn't get it right. The arguing, the silent treatment, and the look of disgust on his face when he looked at me were all becoming too much. The masks started to appear again. I was fasting, I was praying, I was trying, and I was crying, yet things got worse. I remember laying in the bed one night talking to God. And He said to me, "Why don't you pray in your heavenly language?"

I replied, "I don't know God, it sounds funny to me and not right."

God told me to take out my phone and voice text my prayer in my heavenly language. I did that. After I prayed, He said, "Now read it." I started to read it and it didn't make any sense. Below is a journal entry of that voice text:

> *(Journal entry) This is what the devil hears when we speak in tongues...I was praying into my phone, and this is what I got... lol!!! Making a secret sexy little body text Aquino Carlos tasso e Kmart can I watch Metro PCS*

*Pizza Hut Castleton Indiana how many kids
Pizza Hut Delano Buffet Peter Thomas call
Shopify Tulsa Oklahoma Metro PCS Sanibel
siesta Cafe Moda Las Vegas Panama Thomas
Auto Center contact Ashley Krouse Canada.*

God could tell I was confused. He was clear, "That's why you should pray in your heavenly language because when you do, the devil doesn't understand you." That blew my mind! Then, I remembered that speaking in tongues was a new language; and the more you use it, the more it develops. At this stage in my life, I have been praying that way more often. Back then, I noticed that I prayed longer in my heavenly language than I did in English; it was like my spirit had so much to say. I got out the way and let my spiritual tongues have an intimate conversation with God.

I then came upon an obstacle. It seemed like the more I prayed, the harder things got, and I was so confused and angry. I talked to my Christ mentor. "Let's have dinner." She came to my rescue.

We went to dinner, and we talked. She asked, "What's going on?" I started to explain. I'm such a visual and experiential learner that she used those ways to explain things to me. Remember the balloon exercise? She asked, "How long have you been saved?"

I paused. I said, "Well, I got saved at 16. I got baptized at 20. I started to seek God at 25. I started pursuing him about 33, I think."

"You see, the enemy had all that time to study and learn you. He knows your likes and dislikes; he knows how to push your buttons; he knows what makes you react. Every time you react, you are thrown off your path. He knows you. From now on, be aware, think before you react."

I had to understand that I couldn't always blame the enemy and others for the way I responded to life. I had to start taking responsibility. It was my life, and I was responsible for it.

So, I challenge you today to take full responsibility for your life. Stop blaming others for where you are and what you are doing. Look in the mirror; that person that's looking back at you—you owe them everything. Take back your life!

*Reflection page:*

Recall when things were ugly, and you just didn't know which way to go or what to do. Write it out and share how you overcame.

_____

_____

_____

_____

_____

_____

_____

_____

_____

_____

_____

_____

_____

_____

_____

# Reflection

_____

_____

_____

_____

_____

_____

_____

_____

_____

_____

_____

_____

_____

_____

_____

_____

_____

_____

_____

_____

_____

_____

# WORKING TOWARD GREATNESS

By that stage in my life, I felt like I was working toward greatness. There were situations that arose and most of them got a reply or reaction that surprised me.

I started to be more aware of what was happening around me. I became slow to react, if I reacted at all. But the anger inside of me was growing. I was allowing some things to fester, and it wasn't good for my health. I was still praying, and things were still hard, but I refused to give up on prayer this time. I was determined to trust God.

I was in this marriage feeling stuck, my job was horrible, my health was taking a toll on me, and my daughter was having the hardest time in school. I wanted to give up. I wanted to go back to the old me because that seemed to work better. The Christian thing wasn't happening. But I pushed through. There was frustration, lots of anger, and lots of tears. But I kept pushing, praying until something happened.

So, I wasn't going to stop praying and fasting. I know that it was God that helped me through.

On our eighth wedding anniversary, we decided to take a trip. I don't know why because we always argued when we went on anniversary trips. Well, this time we went to St. Augustine, Florida, which was cool because it was somewhere that I had never been. The first day there, we had an issue. That night we had the biggest argument. The saying goes: sticks and stones may break my bones, but words will never hurt. Well, that was a LIE! That was the biggest lie that I had learned in life. Words cut deeper than a knife, words cut to the soul, and penetrate the spirit, if you are not careful.

He said some things that cut me to the core. After the argument, I turned over and began to cry softly. Then, I remembered to not let the enemy see you in distress. I tried to hold the tears, but I couldn't.

God spoke to my spirit, "Go get in the shower." I got up, went to the bathroom, turned on the shower, and got in. When the water hit my body, it was like the well broke. I cried from the core of my soul. The agony of the pain caused me to cry like I had lost the closest person to me, and I had. I had lost myself. I mean, I cried so hard that I was physically weak. I could barely stand, so I leaned against the wall in the shower, then eventually found myself on the floor of the shower crying my eyes out. During that brokenness, I felt a shift in my spirit. While I was crying, I was praying. I was praying as hard as I could. I was crying out to God like never before. Once the shift happened, the tears started to subside. Once I was done crying, I washed up, cleaned my face, and got out. I laid in bed with a sense of peace. In that moment, I wrote this in my phone journal.

> *Today on June 8th, I decided that I'm going to leave my husband. I think that we are two different people, and it would be best if we went our separate ways. It hurts and it breaks my heart, but I must do what's best for me and him. There is a perfect wife out there for him and I pray that God gives him that perfect wife. Jesus, I love you and I thank you for comfort.*

We had a talk the next day and I was so unbothered by anything he had to say or even his mood. I was at peace. It was different because I had never been able to be at peace when it came to him. He always had the ability to shift me in whatever direction he wanted. I believed in that moment I was tired of being a puppet. On June 10<sup>th</sup> I wrote another journal entry.

> *As I lay here at 4:17 am at the Hampton Inn for our anniversary. I think about us. I think this is the beginning of the end. As much as I would like for us to stay together, we are so living and growing in different directions. We had a talk yesterday and he said that I am negative and all I do is complain. There wasn't one thing positive that he could say about me. He told me that he doesn't make me feel good about myself because I'm cocky already and that I'm arrogant. I think that I am going to find me a counselor to get some counseling. I think it would be good for me to go. I'm hurt and I'm broken. I just want to be okay. So, today I vow to love me and make me better. For I am the most important thing in my life to me under God.*

And I did. I started making changes, slowly but surely. I spent the rest of June trying to understand what had transpired. July came and we were going to the water park as a family. On the way, my husband realized that he left his wallet home and somehow that was my fault. That was the day that I HAD IT! I was not going to be the blame for anything anymore. I took my wedding ring off and that was it for my heart.

The next thing was getting out of the marriage and still be pleasing to God. I was taught you don't leave a marriage. The only way out was death. Things were getting tough for me because I wanted out. One night, while lying in bed, I said if death was my only way out then maybe I should end it. It was the night of July 19th. I laid there and I cried, and I contemplated. I didn't cry for me, I cried for my children and my mom. I knew how bad it would hurt them if I killed myself. But the spirit of suicide was so heavy on me. It wasn't a matter of *if* I was going to do it, it was a matter of *how* and *when*. I was waiting for my husband to fall asleep that night so I could take my life. But he would not go to sleep. I started to pray. The next thing I knew, it was morning.

That day I received a phone call from a friend. This was a friend I hadn't talked to in years. They said, "You've been on my mind heavy. What's going on?"

We talked about everything. I was told that I am too precious to a lot of people to leave this earth that way. It meant a lot to me to hear someone say that I am wanted. I vowed to try and love myself. I started to put me first. I wanted a new car, so I started searching online for the perfect one. When I found it, I went to the dealership to see it. I didn't tell them I was coming because I didn't want to be harassed. I searched the lot and there was the car for me. My early birthday present to myself. Since my birthday always falls around Labor Day, I decided to take a girl's trip for the long weekend. It was the best birthday that I had in a long time.

Upon my return, my husband had dinner cooked, a birthday cake, flowers, and gifts waiting for me. It was nice, but I wasn't moved by it. The thing with my husband was he could be an amazing man when he **chose** to be. Life is about choice. You always have two options. Choose well. He had the ability to love, but he often chose not to. I mean this man knew how to make me feel on top of the world at times, and a second later, I would feel down in the valley. Time went on and I was growing and adjusting to my new way of being committed to me. I was still on a rollercoaster with him. Difficulties, twist and turns, highs and lows. I wanted out.

*Lord, I need you! I need you now. God, I pray and leave this marriage and this man up to you, God. Jesus, I need you to touch the heart of this man and his mind. Jesus, I'm asking you to speak to the heart of him. Show him a reflection of himself through a vision, dream, video, or something. Lord, I am asking that if you find him unfaithful, reveal it to me, God. Not just for an out, Jesus, but to help me understand why he treats me the way he does. Lord, now that breaks my heart and bring tears to my eyes because I know I don't deserve to be treated this way. I don't know why he can't love me and appreciate me for who I am. I never thought from a little girl that love would be like this. I know the little girl in me still longs for loving and God, you are doing an AMAZING job and I feel your love, but how come the man I call husband don't love me like you?*

I couldn't figure out why I was the enemy to him. I didn't get it. I was thirty-eight, a wife, a mother of four, in a career, with a new car, a 2900-plus-square foot home and living what you would think was the life. Nope, it wasn't happening like that. By December, I had fasted, prayed, sought all types of advice, and looked for help to save our marriage. I had enough. I prayed to God for my out. I asked God to release me. But it was different this time. It wasn't from a selfish place; it wasn't from a place of anger.

It was from a place of peace and just being tired. When I prayed, I heard God say, "You are released, Daughter." I felt at ease in that moment. Then, the reality of being released started to settle in. I started to think, how? How do I get out? Where do I go? Can I afford an apartment? Do I go stay with family? All these thoughts came rushing to my mind. I had so much to figure out. I wasn't going to let all the unknown consume me, so I moved on with life, following whichever way God was taking me. But there was an internal war going on. Even though I had been saved for a while and following Christ, I was still growing and learning, as I am today. I wondered if I heard God correctly or was it just me. I wondered if I would be out of God's will for leaving or giving up on my marriage. I asked God if He was sure I was released. I laugh now as I type this, asking God was He sure. But I didn't want to mess up. I was trying to get this Christ-following thing right.

No matter how long you have been saved, your walk with God is always different than the next person's. Listen, you are on schedule! Just keep moving, don't stop and don't give up. When you are following God, you are learning as you go. Don't compare yourself to "Super Christians." I did that for years and always felt like a failure in my walk. Seek God for yourself and allow him to lead and guide you.

I was thirty-eight-years-old, and it seemed like my life was falling more apart. I needed something to be excited about. So, I got excited about turning forty. I couldn't wait for the year 2020. I started to make plans for my 40th birthday, something to distract me from leaving home. New Year's Eve night I went to church to bring in the new year.

## HAPPY NEW YEAR!!! 2019

New year, new me! That was the anthem, right? Well, this year had been nothing different from the years before. In October of 2019, our house was broken into. How it happened was all crazy. My youngest son (bonus son) and I left the house later than normal because he had a job interview that morning before school. The interview went well, and he got the job, Yay! I dropped him at school and went to work. Everything was going as planned; it was a regular day. Until I got the phone call. Let me walk you through this series of events. I was sitting at my desk, and I got an urge to post a picture of myself on social media. I posted a picture, and I captioned it, "I know I haven't posted in a while, but I'm still smiling." A minute later I got a text from my middle son in our family chat saying he got pulled over. This is protocol for my sons. When you encounter the police, you send a text and your location. This is our practice since the increase of police killings of unarmed Black men for no reason. I need to know where to arrive or send the closest relative. I was like, "Really? Where? Were you speeding?" No reply. I started to get a little nervous. My oldest son then asked a question, no reply. I started to gather my things. The next text we received from him was someone broke into our house. I said "What!" I called him immediately and he answered, hysterically.

"Are you okay?" I asked.

He replied, "Yeah, I caught him. He was still in the house when I came in."

I jumped up from my desk. "I'm on my way. Go back outside and call the police. DO NOT GO BACK IN THAT HOUSE!"

I was thanking God all the way home that I didn't get a phone call saying something had happened to my son because he walked in on a robbery. I got home and the police were there. I asked my son, "What happened?"

"I was coming in from the garage when I stepped into the house there was a guy in the kitchen heading toward the sliding glass door. When the guy heard me come in, he turned and looked. I screamed, 'what you doin' in my house?' The guy ran out of the sliding glass door, dropping everything he had.

"I ran and locked the sliding glass door and went around the house to chase the guy away."

I almost chocked, "You did what?"

After hearing that story and examining the house, I was so grateful to God for allowing him to get pulled over by a nice cop that didn't harass him and just gave him a ticket for speeding. If he had not gotten pulled over, there was a possibility that he would have walked in on the burglary in action. From the looks of the house, you could tell that there had been more than one person. I mean, every inch of the house was touched. If my son had arrived a few minutes earlier, there may have been a different ending to this part of the story. All I can believe is that God blocked it.

That was a Thursday. That same night, we purchased cameras, and my husband installed them. The next morning, I called and had an alarm system installed and activated on the house. We could tell that the burglars spent hours in our house. Room to room, drawer after drawer. The house was destroyed.

I was perplexed. They had gone in every room in the house, through every drawer in the house, and they used our luggage and laundry bags to pack things in. It was a mess! But because of my son coming home early, some of the things that they had packed, they ended up leaving. All my jewelry was GONE! What hurt the most was the fact that I still had my children's baby jewelry. AND IT WAS GONE! Those things meant a lot to me, and others couldn't understand my heartache, but I'm sure some of you do, right? I was feeling uncomfortable in our own home, but by Thanksgiving things were back to normal. In December, the normal of life as I knew it was getting unbearable for me. I was tired. A friend of mine asked, "Why won't you leave? What are you stuck on?"

I pondered those questions for a while. On December 2nd, I wrote this journal entry...

Title:

I'm not stuck, I'm scared.

On December 10, 2019, the house was broken into, again! EVERYTHING that they didn't get the first time, they got the second time. They came into the house this time where no cameras were pointing, through the office window. I mean, these people had to be watching us put up the cameras to know where there was no coverage. Yep, you guessed it. They destroyed the house, again. It seemed more intentional this time.

THIS WAS UNBELIEVABLE!!! YES, I had an alarm system (by a company I won't name), but it didn't respond to the break in. I was furious, most of all, I was scared. For this to happen a second time in six weeks. This time they also took a firearm out of the house. I didn't know if they were coming back.

The kids and I were terrified that night because we couldn't really assess the damage and exactly what was missing. We all wanted to leave the house for a night. I asked my husband to get a hotel room for the night and we would come back and assess the damages and losses the next day. He refused. I expressed to him that the kids and I were afraid and that we didn't want to stay there that night. He told me that he wasn't leaving and he's not about to allow (a few choice words) to run him away from his house. I understood. But I was only asking for one night. I WAS SPOOKED! But he refused.

I called my older brother and told him that I was scared, and I didn't want to stay there that night. He told me that he was on the phone with my sister-in-law, and he merged me into their call. I told her my daughter and I were on the way to their house because I was scared and asked if I could stay. She welcomed me with open arms. Besides, we were more like sisters than in-laws. I remembered laying on a mattress pad on the floor trying to wrap my brain around what had happened. I was so scared that night. All I wanted my husband to do during that time was to put me first and be there for me. I needed him. I needed him to wrap me in his arms that night and let me know that everything was going to be all right.

I lay there and my eyes started to fill with tears. I still loved him, and I was hoping that something would change between us. I had not shared with him that God had released me. With one blink, I had a streaming line of tears rolling down both cheeks, the flow was constant. I was heartbroken because I just wanted him there with me. I prayed and asked God to wrap me in His arms and hold me tight. The next thing I knew, it was morning. When I opened my eyes and looked at the ceiling, I realized that it wasn't a bad dream. I got up and got myself together. I called my husband, no answer. I was worried because I didn't know if the burglars had come back. I called back, still no answer. I gave it a little bit of time because it was early. I called back around noon and still no answer, I called right back, and he answered. I asked him if he was still sleeping.

"Yeah," was his response.

"Okay, I was calling to see what plan we were going to come up with. Call me when you get up good."

He groggily replied, "Yeah, okay," and hung up.

I took the phone away from my face and looked at it like *I know he didn't just hang up in my face.* It was back to the home screen. I'm not going to lie; my feelings were HURT. I waited all day for him to call me back. There wasn't one call. I knew when he was up because I kept getting camera notifications that there was movement detected. I could see him on the cameras. He never called that day. I figured that he was upset with me because I left. The next day came and went, no call. By then, I wanted to see if he was going to call me like I asked him to, so I didn't call him. Every night I cried because I couldn't believe that he didn't care. I was thinking, he knew I left upset and scared, and he was not going to check on me. Another two days passed. It had been a total of four days since I had heard from my husband. Four days! He was that upset that it took him four days to reach out to me. I was mad! In those four days, I did some self-searching and asked God a lot of questions. Questions like, "Was I wrong for leaving home? Was I wrong for being afraid? Did I move too quickly? Should I have sucked up my feelings and pushed through?"

I asked God, "Why wasn't my husband concerned about me? Should I call?" At that point, I knew I didn't want to go back home. And I didn't. From that day to the time of me writing this book, I have not lived in that house again, the house I loved so much. For five months, I lived with my sister and brother. Over that time, so much happened. There is one memory that spooked me after the whole break-in thing. My daughter was slacking in school. I was going to take her phone from her, but somehow she broke her phone, and I wasn't going to get another one until Christmas. Didn't stick to that plan. My daughter started playing basketball for her school, abruptly. One day they needed a player, and they asked her to play. She said she called me, and I didn't answer.

She called her dad and asked him if she could play in the game. He told her yes. I knew nothing about this.

I got a call from my mom asking, "Did Nae go to school today?"

"Yes?" I responded with questioning in my voice, I guess she could hear it because she responded to my tone.

"It's past time for her to be here, and we can't find her."

There was a pause because I was replaying what she had said to me. My heart felt as if it stopped, instantly.

"What you mean y'all can't find her?" I questioned, as I wrapped my brain around what she said to me.

Mom started to explain, "Once she wasn't here, Bell (my dad) went to look for her, and he didn't see her anywhere."

I was about to lose my mind. She continued, "He's going to go look again. I will call you back."

I had a blank stare on my face. My co-worker asked, "Shay, what's wrong?"

"They can't find my baby." My heart started to race; I ran out of the front to my office. I paced the floor and started praying.

This happened during the heightened child trafficking period.

My mom called back, "We can't find her."

I grabbed my things and told them, "I HAVE TO GO!" I ran out of the building.

I was praying and talking to God the whole time I was driving. I knew I had to call her dad and tell him. I was hesitant. I called my husband hoping he wouldn't answer right away, but he answered.

I swallowed hard. I began to talk to him very cautiously and made sure that the tone of my voice wasn't off. I asked him a couple of questions first. "Are you busy? How's your day going?" He replied to the questions seeming to be in a good space.

I then said, "We can't find Nae."

"What you mean?" he responded.

I told him, "Mom just called me and said that they can't find her. She didn't come home from school, and they rode all over the neighborhood and they can't find her."

He then says, "Oh, she's at her basketball game."

I forgot for a moment that I was driving as I talked to him. Everything seemed to have stopped, and I was completely silent. Tears filled my eyes as I held my breath trying not to scream to the top of my lungs. I released the deepest sigh and I felt relieved. I blinked my eyes and the tears started to run down my cheeks. I pulled over to gather myself. He was still talking, but I didn't hear anything he said. I was so relieved that my baby was safe, all I could do was cry.

"What? You didn't know?"

"I have to go." I released the call.

I called my parents because they were as nervous as I was not knowing my daughter's whereabouts. When I called my mom and told her where my daughter was, she was relieved, but she had a thousand questions. I answered what I could on my way back to work. When I parked, I sat in the car and cried. It was a cry of gratitude to God that my baby was safe. I had never been that scared in my life. With all the things that had happened in my life, that was by far the scariest moment.

That night when I left work, I went straight to the store and purchased a phone for her. When I arrived at my parents' house to pick her up, I was more relieved to physically see her face. It was a feeling I can't put into words. For days after that I would think back to the moment, and I would get teary eyed. I empathize with all the parents that have ever had or currently have a missing child.

2019 was such a mess! I couldn't wait until 2020. I was hoping that 2020 would be different. For the first time in years, I brought in the new year alone. I was at church with a room full of people, but I wasn't with my family. I felt lonely. After the countdown, I was out! I left in a hurry. I was hurting, and I didn't want to be around anyone. My truth was settling in. I was separated from my husband. I talked to God all the way home. Home was still at my brother and sister's house. When I got home, I wrote this journal entry.

*Titled Silent cries:*

*When the tears roll down my cheeks without a word, please hear my silent cry. When my eyes well up and I won't let a tear drop, please hear my silent cry. When my voice trembles when I try to express how I feel, please hear my silent cry. When I'm asked what's wrong and I reply I'm okay, please hear my silent cry. I cry from hurts, I cry from pain, I cry when I'm angry, I cry from disappointments, I cry when I'm overwhelmed, I cry when I'm frustrated. You may not always see my tears, but please hear my silent cry. I was told every tear is bottled so there is a collection for me. More bottles than I count, but He hears my silent cries...*

I always keep a journal near so I can write in the moment. I've learned that writing in the moment allows you to deal with it and get what's in you onto paper. Even when I can't find the words to formulate sentences, I just write whatever words come to mind. The more I journal, the better I feel. I recommend this to others that have a hard time expressing themselves or opening up to others. If you can't be honest with yourself, who can you be honest with? It starts with self.

We were a few days into the new year when my husband's grandmother passed away. This hurt me because she was one of the few that really treated me like family. We had some conversations that I will cherish forever. I didn't know how to tell my daughter. She loved her great grandmother. She passed two days before my daughter's birthday. I thought to myself that was how the year was going to start. My husband and I decided not to tell her until after her birthday. That was the hardest thing to keep from her. It was only a couple of days, but those days seemed like weeks. We told her and she was shocked, but she took it well.

I made it through the funeral. I tried to be strong for my kids and my husband through the service.

The gravesite was something different. When we got to the end of the burial service, I couldn't take it. I couldn't be strong anymore. I walked to the truck, got in, and let out a wail from my soul. I cried so hard I couldn't breathe. I allowed myself to cry it all out. That one was rough for me. A few days later I was on Facebook messenger, and Dr. Loneryl "Dee" Reid's profile picture came up. And God said, "Now. Now is the time to reach out to start counseling." I was obedient. I started counseling weekly. The first couple of sessions were venting sessions. I talked and talked. That was great. There was someone unbiased to listen to all my problems. That's what counseling was, right? Much to my surprise. That wasn't all there was to inner healing. We started to dig beneath the surface of things. Let me be completely honest right here...I didn't think that I was ready to let someone that I didn't know into spaces within myself that I protected. I started not being completely open; I kept my guard up. I had been dropped so many times by people that I didn't think this would be much different. I would give her just enough information that I could keep myself protected. One day I was lying in the bed, talking to the Lord. "God this counseling thing is not helping."

God said to me, "It would really work if you were honest with yourself and your counselor." I started to search myself. I realized that getting healed was going to take work. I said to myself, "So, you are going to pay someone to help you heal, but not allow them to help you." In that moment, I decided to trust my counselor. I confessed to her about me not being completely open and honest with her because I didn't want to be dropped or really uncover the things that I had learned to live with for years. She told me she knew; she was waiting for me to be ready.

We finished out January strong. I was healing and getting back to life. Then, BOOM! My father-in-law died unexpectedly. This one didn't hit as hard for me because we didn't have a great relationship. But what I had to talk to God about after his death was the unforgiveness that I held on to. The hard part about this was I had to forgive him in his death. Despite that, I was there for my husband and brother-in-law every step of the way. This was a challenging time. I was so glad that I was in counseling, although counseling was getting tough, we started uncovering things. I was getting homework assignments, mostly consisting of questions that required a written answer. One of my homework assignment questions was:

Why do I give myself permission to heal? This question was one that I pondered for days. It was something I had to think about. And because I thought it wasn't an acceptable answer for my counselor, it instead became a journal entry...

> *I know what permission means, but as I look up the definition, it's to give consent, authorization. I still need to look further so I looked up synonyms for permission. It says the same. I needed more so I looked up the thesaurus. It gave me related words and synonyms. It said accepting, acknowledgment, acquiring, admission, agreement, then this word APPROVAL.*
>
> *Approval is something I have longed for, for most of my life. So, I changed the question a little.*
>
> *WHY DO I APPROVE MYSELF TO HEAL?*
>
> *For the longest time approval is something I've always wanted. I always wanted to prove that I am good enough.*
>
> *Don't leave me, don't walk away, watch, I am good enough!*

*I've wanted to prove this to everyone, mostly the men in my life. Even though God asked, "Why do you need validation from man when I validate you." The more I heard it, the more I believed it. But there was a small something in the pit of my soul that I needed to align with. It was self-approval.*

*I approve myself to heal because I deserve it. I approve myself to heal because I don't want to live in my past. I no longer want my past to control me. I approve myself to heal because I want my fullness of Joy. I approve myself to heal because I want to feel whole instead of shattered pieces. I approve myself to heal because I no longer want to bleed on people who did not cut me. I approve myself to heal so I can help heal others. I approve myself to heal so I can walk boldly in my truth. I approve myself to heal so I can love and be loved. I approve myself to heal because after healing, life starts. I approve myself to heal so I can forgive myself. I give myself permission to heal so that I can be SOUND AND HEALTHY. The definition of heal. I give myself permission to heal so that I can heal-thy self (healthy). Last reason is because I love me, and I want to be the best version of myself in this second half...*

I was scared to see what March was going to bring in counseling and in the world. I was looking forward to pulling some more of the waste out of my system. I had other assignments, but the next one that stuck out was writing a letter to my younger self. It took me weeks to even start that letter. Every week, I continued to go to counseling. Dr. Dee would ask, "Have you started the letter?"

I would drop my head and sit in silence for a minute. "No, ma'am" was my reply. She would always say, "When you're ready, you will." My next assignment was claiming back my pieces. My pieces to life and my pieces from trauma. This was hard for me. I had two assignments, and I didn't know where to start with either. Counseling was weekly, so I knew I couldn't go back with nothing. I decided I would write the letter to my younger self. Once I started writing the letter, I was able to start claiming my pieces. I wasn't finished with it yet, but the letter to myself revealed some things that made me take a closer look within.

*Hey baby girl, I'm sorry I left you there but returning to you caused me so much fear. Wondering would you accept me, hoping that you listen and understand, praying you give me a chance to explain. Let me start with saying I miss you and having you with me through these years would have helped me make better decisions. I'm sorry for leaving you when daddy left, I'm sorry for leaving you when he abandoned you. I'm sorry for leaving you to fight on your own when you were bullied by adults. I'm sorry. I'm sorry for giving our innocence away when we weren't ready. Forgive me. I left you many times and you would always fight to come along, but I felt the need to protect you. You've been hurt so many times before and I couldn't bear to take you along this rollercoaster ride called life. And because I didn't, I abandoned you on so many levels and so many ages. But I tried protecting you. I didn't want you to hurt anymore so I thought that walls were best for you. If I can protect you, then no one could hurt you ever again. Which was a mistake and I'm sorry. Because if I had allowed us to band together, we could have conquered these obstacles together. I love you and you mean the world to me so I will take these blows from life for you. Many times, I wanted to end it all and tried to because I wasn't strong enough, but then I remembered you. I remembered how strong you were as a six-year-old girl standing there while you were being crushed without a tear. I remembered how strong you were when you felt like your life had no meaning. I remembered how strong you were when you were left to be a parent on your own at the tender age of 16. I remembered. I remembered all the times you stood up for yourself and I left you. Left you in that stage of life and built a shield around you. I watched you give your life to the Lord at 16 and I still felt the need to protect you. Walls, brick walls were the best protection, I thought. At age 19, I left you to fight the rapist off yourself, I left you. And I'm sorry. Abandoning you became easier than helping you heal from trauma.*

I stopped at the age of 19. I was digging deep within. I couldn't write anymore. I knew that it was something that I had to finish, and I planned to. But going back to those places was like reliving those moments. I felt all the emotions as if they were happening right at that moment. While working on the letter to myself, I was able to reclaim some of my pieces. This is how that went…

> **Daddy**, *I forgive you and I'm calling my heart back and returning to you, abandonment.*

> **Tweety**, *I forgive you and I'm calling back my ability to love, wholeheartedly. I'm calling back my trust for others. I'm calling back my heart from you, and I'm returning to you, abandonment.*

> **Clarence**, *I forgive you, and I'm calling back my strength you took from me. I'm calling back my confidence you stole from me. I'm calling back my innocence you ripped from me. I'm calling back my life from that trauma you took me through. I return to you, fear. I return to you that spirit of lust.*

March came in without bringing death to the family; but then, the 2020 Coronavirus pandemic started. This became a different kind of life for everyone. I was still in counseling, but it was virtual. Funny because I didn't think that I would get anything not being in the office. Much to my surprise, it was still as powerful. I made it through April and May, but by June, God told me I had to stop all communication. I didn't believe that it was God because He knew that I was seeking Him for things. I was used to Him answering me but giving me confirmation through someone else. But I was obedient. I stopped talking to my family, friends, mentors, everyone. It was difficult because I couldn't talk to anyone about anything. It was difficult because I relied on my friends to keep me going. I felt like I needed them to get through because I was lonely. Before I completely cut communication, I asked one of my friends if she had a Word for me from God. She said, "God said that this is between you and Him." I was not happy, but I knew what she was talking about. I knew then that I heard correctly; I was supposed to shut up in that season. I lost relationships that I thought were unshakable. God showed Himself to me while in my silence. I couldn't ask anyone for confirmation. I had to trust and believe for myself, by myself. For instance, one night I was crying and missed my life with my husband and having my own space. I was laying in the bed, talking to God about it.

I said to God, "God, if you tell me to go home right now, I will pack all my stuff and be there in the

morning. But if you tell me to be still, I will be still."
It wasn't 10 minutes later that my sister came to the
door. "Hey, I was just checking on you."

"Yeah, I'm just laying here trying to figure out life."
I started to explain. She stood quietly and listened.
When I was done, she said, "Sis, I think that you
should 'be still'."

I got chills when she used those words. Because
those were the words I had just used with God. I
looked at her and whispered, "Okay." She walked
away, and I turned over and cried silently.

"Okay God, I heard you," I cried out. The next
day I asked her what made her come in the room
and check on me.

"I don't know, something just nudged me to come
check on you." For me that was further confirmation
to the words *be still*.

In the middle of the pandemic, I felt varying emotions, hoping that it would be over soon. I was crying
out to God like, "Lord, I need you! I need to see
you, I need to hear from you, I need you to help me
because I can't do this on my own." I was at a point
where I had to spend time with me. I hadn't been
it this place in years. I mean, I was always praying,
fasting, worshipping, praising, and going to church.

But in this place, it was something different, I was RESPONSIBLE. I was responsible for my prayers, my fasting, there was no praise team to usher me into worship, there was no one to remind me to praise, there was no church building to go to because everything was shutdown. IT WAS ALL UP TO ME! In that space was where my relationship with God shifted once more. I WAS MY ACCOUNTABILITY PARTNER. In that space, I started to learn about myself all over again.

One thing that I discovered there was that I was lost, and I didn't truly know myself. That's when the breaking started to happen. I asked God, "How and why? How and why are you breaking me when I'm already broken?" Then, I remembered that sometimes something broken must be reset and that required a break and a shift. I cried. I cried because everything that I set out to accomplish by forty, I had done it. And by that time, everything was in reverse. I felt like I was losing everything that I held dear to my heart. IT WASN'T SUPPOSED TO BE THIS WAY! As days passed, things were lonely. I cried a lot, and I prayed a lot. I was working from home because of the pandemic so I didn't have to hide my true feelings. I often cried during the day. I went through a washing of my soul and spirit. I couldn't talk to anyone because I was in a season of SHUT UP. Because I liked to talk and share everything that I thought was worth sharing. This was hard for me, but I was obedient. I would start sharing and I would hear God say, "You're talking." I couldn't even share with my momma. This was the hardest part because I told her A LOT.

Things were getting heavy. God was doing and showing me things right before my eyes. The more I was in tune with God, the more things were revealed. I was in awe of the things I started to see. MAN, GOD IS REAL! He started to reveal people and show me stuff that I never saw, although it had been in my face the entire time. I began talking to God all day, we had deep conversations. He became all I needed and wanted. There was my shift. I stopped carrying everything and started giving Him everything.

One night I was talking to God about life and how everything was shifting and falling apart (my vision). I missed seeing my children because they weren't coming to visit often. My son was from pillar to post because he still didn't feel comfortable in the house. It really bothered me. I told God I needed a place to stay. I told Him, I needed a place to call home for me and my children. I needed somewhere for my son to lay his head and feel comfortable. I was specific when I prayed. I told Him I needed a place in a quiet neighborhood, not far away from my job because I was tired of the commute. I needed it to be affordable. I went to sleep and left the requests with God. The next day I got a call from my uncle. I was sleeping when the phone rang; I looked at it but didn't answer because I figured he was just checking on me and going to lecture me about my marriage and the importance of working on it. So, I put the phone down. God said, "Call him back now."

So, I woke up and called him back in obedience, even though I didn't want to.

He answered, "Hey, how are you?"

"I'm good." I answered with sleep still in my voice.

"Did I wake you?"

I said, "Yes sir, but it's okay."

"Are you still looking for somewhere to stay or you going back home?"

I'm thinking, *oh boy, here we go.* "No, I'm still looking."

"Okay, well I have my big house coming up for rent. It's a six bed, two bath."

I fully woke up by this time. "Really! Where is it located?"

He told me.

"That sounds perfect. How much is the rent?"

He told me. I asked to look at it.

He replied, "Well, meet me over there tomorrow about 6 pm."

He gave me the address and I was immediately excited. Then it dawned on me. I didn't have anything to move with. Not even a bed to sleep on. I started to worry. I started talking to God about it, and I heard the voice of the Lord say, "Haven't I always provided for you?"

In that moment, I was done worrying. I went the next day to look at the house with my kids. The location was perfect, and the neighborhood looked quiet. We went inside of the house, and I instantly saw how I could make that house a home. The boys WERE NOT IMPRESSED. It did need a little tender loving care, but it wasn't anything that I couldn't do.

My uncle and I stood on the porch and talked; he offered to decrease the rent for me. It was Everything that I asked God for. He allowed me to start working on the house two weeks before we moved in. And we made that house our home. We would be living in a fully furnished six-bedroom, two-bathroom house with a bonus room and bathroom in the back. God provided! When I think about God's goodness and how He is constantly shining on me, I get overwhelmed with joy. I say all that to say this, as I penned this chapter, it was September 2nd, the day before my 40th birthday and I am still here!

*On this journey to greatness!!!!*

# TRUST THE PROCESS!

I n the process, I was finding peace. I say "finding" because every day was, and still is a new day of choice. Life is about making a choice to do or not to do. I wake up and I choose peace, I choose love, I choose happiness. In this process of learning about myself, I have learned that there are things we hold on to that will rob us of our choice. I realized in my process that unforgiveness and fear had robbed me of making the choice to be happy and at peace. I allowed moments to control hours, days, weeks, months, and even years of my life. God was and is very strategic.

I am an educator. I had worked in the same school for ten years. That school had been through a lot. To give you an idea, the school had sixteen administrators in the ten years that I was employed there. Every summer I was going to quit this job because this was a hard school to work in. Well, in 2021, we got a new principal. She was initially the assistant principal.

However, this lady came off as the sweetest person in the world, while stabbing you in the back at the same time. I thought it was just me, but everyone shared the same sentiment about her. I wanted to leave for several reasons, but she became the main one. It got so bad that I would get angry on my way to work. I would get there and sit in the car for a while and pray before I entered the school. I was getting myself ready to play the, "I like you, you like me" game. One day I was sitting at my desk, contemplating working with her for the upcoming school year. My chest started to hurt, so I switched positions in the chair. My breaths started to become short, I tried to take deeper breaths and blow them out through my mouth. I started to feel this heaviness. I placed my hands on my chest and my heart was beating fast. I called for help, but no one was available to come to me. I called the school nurse and told her what was going on with me and that I was leaving. I got in my car and started to head home. When I got down the street, these big tear drops started to fall. My chest was hurting, I was having a tough time breathing, and now the tear drops. I was praying over myself as I was driving because now, I was scared. By the time I reached my driveway, I was screaming and crying.

My chest felt like a pound of bricks was on it and I couldn't breathe. My hands were starting to tremble. I picked up the phone and called the doctor. When the nurse answered, I could barely get my name out. She advised me that I was having an anxiety attack. She asked where I was.

I told her, "Home."

She then put me on hold. She came back to the phone and said, "I need you to get to your prescription and take one of your pills and lay down. Can you do that?"

I said, "I think so."

She said, "I'm going to get the doctor and call you back in 30 minutes."

I did exactly what she told me to do. She called back, and I was half asleep. She asked a series of questions. I told her that I was still having chest pains. She told me that they should go away and if they did not go away within an hour to call back.

I fell asleep and when I woke up it was 7pm. My first anxiety attack in 40 years and all because I was thinking about working with that principal. That night the fear of moving on wasn't as heavy. I started applying for other teaching jobs. I went on six interviews, and I was offered five of the six jobs I applied for. The fear was gone; I knew it when I was able to walk away from my job that had become stressful. It took a health scare for me to make a move. Once I secured one of the positions, I handed in my resignation. The soul ties to that job were broken. I felt free! My last day was Friday, July 7th. That Monday I went back in to help them with some reporting that needed to be done. I was already kicked out of the system, so I couldn't help. I told the principal to let me know when I had access again so that I could come in and help. That Tuesday morning, I messaged her and asked, "Any updates?"

She responded, "Not yet, I will let you know when I hear something."

"Okay."

I started to talk to God about some matters. Unrelated to what we were talking about, He said, "You have to forgive them."

"Who, God?"

"Your husband," He replied.

I thought I had done that, but I was obedient. Then God said, "Your daddy and his wife."

*Wait a minute, God!* I took a deep breath, and I sat on the side of my bed. I called my husband and I started to talk. I told him all the things I forgave him for, and I apologized for my role in our difficult relationship. He was quiet the whole time I was talking. When I was done, he said, "Thank you. Thank you for forgiving me."

I told him what happened between God and me and how it prompted me to make that phone call. I shared with him that I had to call and forgive my dad and his wife as well. He asked, "Are you ready for that?"

I told him, "I have no choice. I have held on to this hurt and unforgiveness long enough and it's time to let go. It's keeping me from growing."

I ended the conversation with my husband. I wanted to call my dad, but fear wouldn't let me. I decided to send a text message. In the text message I told him that I forgave him, and the tears flowed. I told him all the specific things that I forgave him for. The more I typed, the more I cried. At the end of my text, I told him to tell his wife I forgave her too. The minute I pressed send it was like the flood gates opened. I sat on the side of the bed with my head in my hands, trying to control the tears. I didn't want to cry about my daddy issues at 40 years old! But when I stopped resisting the emotions and allowed myself to cry and feel all the feelings I needed to, that's when I started to heal. In that process, I heard God say, "This will be the last time you cry about this."

At that moment, I felt the vibration of my phone. I hesitated to look, but I knew it was my dad. When I picked up my phone, there was a text message that read, "You need to call me, you got it wrong." Once I read the text message, I knew I had to take that next step and have the conversation. The little girl inside me was trembling with fear. The adult me had to assure her that it would be okay and that we needed to have this conversation. I got myself together, and I called him. The minute he said, "Hello," the tears started again.

"Are you crying?" He asked.

I couldn't talk, so I didn't answer. He allowed me to cry for a couple minutes. He was so patient with me. "I need you to breathe," he encouraged.

I tried taking deep breaths. He continued, "I need you to get yourself together."

I was trying to control the tears and my breathing at the same time. It was completely silent on his end. Once I stopped crying, my dad asked, "Are you okay?"

I took a deep breath again and replied, "Yeah, I think so."

He started to talk and responded to everything I texted him. He asked questions, I asked questions and he responded to the little girl inside of me dealing with daddy issues. By the end of the conversation, we were having an adult conversation that was needed for my healing. After we got off the phone, I felt physically lighter. It was like waste was removed from my body. Unforgiveness weighs your body down, physically, mentally, and emotionally. Trust me—let it go! It's worth it.

I'm learning in life, to feel feelings because blocking them causes unhealthy habits. One of my favorite things was to build walls on the inside of myself. With each trauma, there was a wall. These walls had ruined and ended many relationships in my life. There were so many layers to me that it was hard to allow anyone in. I wanted to trust, but I couldn't. I wanted to love, wholeheartedly but I couldn't. I wanted to give 100% to a lot of things, but the walls that I built within wouldn't allow me to. I thought I had to protect me, but all the while God was protecting me. He allowed it all. It was to mold me and grow me into the woman that I am today. RESTORED!

If He did it for me, He will do it for you. I AM A WORK IN PROGRESS.

To continue my healing process, I started to take more accountability for me and my actions. The more I understood that life is about choices, I chose to work on my choices daily. I went on a 40 day fast with God for clarity and direction, and my life took another shift. After I finished the fast, I felt accomplished because it was something that I had never done. One of my close friends always says to get something you never had you have to do something you've never done. I started to believe that I wanted to live outside the box. I also believed that every encounter with God changes our lives.

A few weeks later, the number 12 was floating all around me and I asked God—"Why 12?" I asked a few friends who were using the number 12 for various things, why that number. Each friend said that is what God gave them. That number was heavy on my mind, and it was doing something to my soul. I couldn't get the number off my mind.

I asked God again, "Why 12?"

He answered, "Completeness."

He told me that He wanted me to do a 12-week fast, and I questioned Him about that. With little understanding, and fear of failing, I said, "Okay, Lord."

I started the journey. I didn't know what to do but seek God for direction. He gave me the instructions I sought. There were so many things that He told me, but the hardest part for me was focusing on me and only me for the next 12 weeks. I took out my phone and I entered the 12 weeks on my calendar. When I saw how far it went on my calendar, I instantly felt defeated. But I knew that I heard God, and He wasn't going to let me fail. The day before I started this journey, I sat with God hoping, again, that I heard Him wrong, and He was going to correct me. NOPE! That didn't happen. Instead, He gave me a blueprint. I was so overwhelmed with starting this journey alone and ending it alone. I realized that it was all necessary.

Twelve is found in the Bible in 187 places. With 22 occurrences of the number in the book of Revelation. The number is a perfect number. It symbolizes God's power and authority, it also symbolizes a perfect foundation, according to Biblestudy.org.

On June 19, 2022 (Father's Day), I set out on a 12-week journey with just me and God. I've been told that in your obedience comes great sacrifice and with great sacrifice comes great rewards. There were some good days, hard days, and very emotional days, but I made it. I was always the one in the circle that had a lack of confidence for who I am in Christ. I knew that I was called, and I knew that I was chosen, but now I KNOW without a doubt.

I didn't feel like I was as anointed as others, and I didn't think that I prayed like others, and I didn't think God really had a plan for me in ministry. I thought that I would always be the support system. In those 12 weeks, my life shifted to another level in Christ. When I started, I was searching for something on the inside of me that felt like it was missing but I couldn't put a name to it. I thought it was love, but love was always there. I thought it was belonging, but I belonged wherever God was. But there was something that I was searching for on the inside of me that needed to be birthed. The first day of the journey felt like foreign territory, but at the same time, it felt familiar, like God and I had done this so many times.

Day One, I started strong! I spent time with God, I journaled, and wrote down how I felt. Days Two and Three, same thing, I was on top of it. After Day Four, I thought *just everyday life*, I didn't really feel like journaling or making time to do it.

Well, what I didn't know is that my "YES" to this fast gave God something to work with. You see, we expect God to do all these things in our lives, but we don't give Him our "Yes." There are things that God wants to release in the land for us, but it comes with obedience and sacrifice, and I learned that more on my fasting journey. There were so many things that happened - big and small - and I didn't capture them all with journaling. But on September 09, 2022, I had a conversation with one of my sisters in Christ. This sister I had never met in person, just phone calls and Zoom meetings. When I heard her voice that day, I knew exactly who she was. I was excited to finally meet her. I greeted her with a hug. I forgot that she was coming to a conference I was attending. But God has His way of making things come together. There was an issue that came up and we needed to go on a store run. One of the women, Maureen, and I said that we would go. As we were driving to the store, we were conversing about a lot, just trying to get it all in.

She was sharing an encounter that she had with God. And I was so intrigued by what she was telling me. There was so much, but this one part stuck out to me. She said that in the chest cavity there are so many holes, as if the person had been shot and she was praying, but the holes wouldn't close. There were still fragments in the holes and if the holes would close there would still be residue and the person wouldn't be able to heal properly. I was agreeing with the revelation in the story, and we were excited about this conversation. She shared that God revealed to her that she was to imagine that she saw, and to understand that He didn't want to simply heal her, He wanted to make her whole. That was a shouting point for me! As I wrote these words, I realized that God removed the fragments from my wounds over those 12 weeks to make me whole. Because there is a difference between being healed and being made whole. Wholeness is where the wounds are cleansed from infection and the residue of the past. There was residue that God needed to go in and cleanse me of before I could go to my next level in him, before I could finish this book, before I could move forward in life.

Strategically, the conference Maureen and I were attending was called "Behind the Mask." The speaker's topic for that night was "Unbelief." This was something that I struggled with before those 12 weeks. The speaker said, "There are two reasons that we don't believe: 1) You don't believe what God said, or 2) You don't believe who God is." What a way to bring my fast to a close.

As I am writing and thinking back to the 12 weeks, I think about how I started on Fathers' Day and ended with a conference called "Behind the Mask."

God told me that He would make my enemies my footstool and He did just that. When I say footstool, I am not talking about somewhere you rest your feet, I am talking about how your enemies will return to you humbly and ask for your forgiveness and apologize for the pain that they have caused. God told me that He wanted me to focus on meekness. And I thought, *God, I ain't no punk!* But I was obedient. And in my obedience, God delivered. There were people who I thought I would never speak to again who came to me, apologized, and asked for my forgiveness. It blows my mind because in my healing process, I had to forgive those people without an apology. From friends that betrayed me to men who hurt me.

I was two weeks away from finishing my 12 weeks and God had blown my mind over and over. I told Him that I am in awe of all the things He has shown me and done for me. I was satisfied and ready to end my fast. Well, Week 11 was my birthday week, and I was feeling free, light, and refreshed. My husband and I had been separated for two and half years. He asked if he could take me out of town for my birthday because he needed to get away and I wanted too as well. I told him, "Sure, I just have one requirement."

He asked "What's that? "

"I want to wake up to water."

"Okay, done."

That Friday, September 2, 2022, we left for our trip. My husband was always a great planner, so I trusted him with making great choices for our stay. After a couple of hours of driving, we pulled up to this beautiful hotel, off the water. I looked at him with a smile. *Oh, he's trying to impress me.* He checked in as bellhops unpacked his truck. I went inside to the room on the fifth floor, where I was able to oversee the ocean at the perfect height. I spent hours on the balcony just talking to God and spending time with my husband. Friday ended, and I was happy. Saturday was MY BIRTHDAY!!! September 3, 2022 is a day I will never forget. We got up, got dressed, and hit the street. Starting with breakfast, then the nail shop for pedicures, then shopping. Store after store, we shopped and browsed. I was tired. I needed a nap. When we got back to the room, I again went to talk with God on the balcony, thanking Him for that day. I then showered and crashed. My husband followed suit. I slept a few hours and when I woke up it was dusk outside. I eased out of bed and sat, again, on the balcony. Eventually, he woke up and I could see him moving around in the room, but I didn't pay attention. Finally, he joined me on the balcony, and we talked.

He asked, "How was your day?"

I told him that I didn't have a complaint and that he did a great job, and I thanked him. He smiled.

After people-watching and laughing, he went inside, so I followed. To my surprise, there was a purse that I wanted from one of the stores, but I didn't get it.

I exclaimed, "How did this get here?" I started to laugh. "You are slick!" I chuckled.

He laughed and asked, "What are you talking about?"

I was so excited, so I know that I was talking loudly. I asked, "When and how did you get this pass me?"

I picked up the purse, and it was unusually heavy. I looked at him and he had a smile on his face. I opened the purse, and it was loaded with other gifts. There were birthday cards and perfume. I felt something in the zipped-up pocket on the inside of the purse. I unzipped the pocket and I saw a box. I pulled the box out and I sat it to the side because I thought to myself, *I am not doing this with him.*

I opened and read the first card. It was really sweet. I opened the second one and the words on the card spoke directly to our situation. I started to cry my heart out. I thought, *why did we have to go through all the mess we endured throughout our entire relationship only to get to this place, in the hotel room where he was about to do what I never thought he would do?* I wiped my tears and removed my hands from my face. My husband was down on one knee with the box open.

I looked at the ring as he asked, "Shay, will you marry me, again?"

# Reflection page

_____

_____

_____

_____

_____

_____

_____

_____

_____

_____

_____

_____

_____

_____

_____

_____

_____

_____

_____

# Reflection page

# HOW MY JOURNEY ENDED

I want to share with you my final journal entry from September 11, 2022, the last day of my 12 weeks of planned encounters with God.

I decided a few weeks ago that the best way for me to end my fast is in my favorite place. As I got turned around this morning, I didn't get frustrated. I made a few turns and got myself back on track. I noticed that life is that way. We set out to go one way and before we know it, we are headed in a different direction. BUT with a few adjustments we can get back on track, to the purpose and plan that God has for us.

After making the adjustments, I was headed to the beach. The drive was normal, and my mood was at peace, once I exited the interstate and started down the Causeway, the sun started to rise behind me, and I felt covered. I couldn't wait to get to the beach to meet God because I knew he was waiting for me. The closer I got to the beach the more I anticipated meeting Him there. As I'm driving, I looked out the window to my left and I saw a rainbow. I started to smile because I knew that my spot is where I was supposed to complete my final journal entry. I looked to the right and the other end of the rainbow was there and very bright. I knew that I was in the right place; it was like God was saying, "Welcome daughter, I've been waiting for you." When I parked, I couldn't help but have a Kool-Aid smile because I felt the love. I'm so analytical so I need signs and wonders and the rainbow was the sign of being in the right place. This relationship with God brings life to me, it means the world to me. I just want to take a moment and thank God for being great. Thank You, Lord for your mercy. Lord, Thank You for your love and patience with me. God, Thank You for life!

It's something about having planned encounters with God that change the game for me. He looks forward to meeting with me as much as I look forward to meeting with him. I have waited all my life to feel this level of love and as I grow and get closer to God, I realize that no man or woman on earth has the ability to love me like God. He was always there, just waiting to give me what He had for me. There is this song called "This Place" by Gospel artist, Tamela

Mann. The words to that song resonate with me in this part of my life. It says that "I never knew that my heart would feel again." It says "I never thought the tears would go away. I never knew that I could be in this place where the sun shines all day." To be made whole is indescribable and it brings happy tears to my eyes because I never thought that I would be the one without hurt. I never thought that I would be the one able to forgive so easily. I didn't know that I would be able to love again without restrictions. I didn't know that taking off the mask allows me to feel. I feel feelings y'all. It's been over 25 years since I really allowed myself to feel. I was numb and heavy all those years, I can feel the difference now that I have let go. I feel so much lighter, physically, mentally, and emotionally. I feel youthful. I went back to get me from all the stages I left myself. I forgave me and I learned to trust me fully; me, with all my flaws and insecurities. When I made up in my mind that I wanted the fullness of my life and decided to work on me, my life changed, and it is forever changing.

When I think about this place, it took me years to get here, it wasn't an overnight fix and I had to fight to get here. I refused to live in the bondage of *what if*. I had a strong tribe behind me pushing me and who wouldn't allow me to retreat even when the water was neck deep. They told me to keep going because God wouldn't let me drown and even though it felt like He had left me, and I was going to drown, I had to remember that He is a teacher and teachers don't always talk during a test. A test is placed before us so that we can put into place what we've learned. So, at times of tests, I can hear God telling me, "Right here, baby girl, is where you practice what I have taught you in this season." Once the test is passed, I see the other side where the blessing awaits me. What's different now is that when I'm going through a test, I know that the Lord is rooting for me. It's almost like a boxing match. When the trainer is on the side of the ring and he's yelling, "left, left, right, duck, jab, jab!" and you are listening and following directions and it keeps you in the fight. And you are just waiting for the bell to ring because you feel that you don't have another swing. And just when you want to give up, the bell rings. You go into your corner with your bumps and bruises. You're bleeding and sweating because you are in the fight of your life and the trainer tells you how well you are doing and that it is almost the 12th round. He gives you a little water and sends you back out into this world to fight a little more. Before you know it, it's the 12th round and the final bell rings and you are still standing. You look to the hills, and He tells you I knew you had it all the time. It gives you another level of confidence.

Trusting God in the waters is easier said than done, but if you just try it, you will see it gets easier with every level of tide. When the water gets into your ears, I know you may grow a little nervous because I do, but if you just doggy pedal through the high tides, you will get to the other end. It may take you a little while, but the goal is to keep going and don't stop even when you're tired because you will drown. Make sure you have a group a people around you that are strong swimmers until you are a Michael Phelps. I know that sometimes we want to walk through this life alone because it seems easier, but you need somebody. You see the trick of the enemy will have you thinking that this life was designed to be done alone when you've been hurt, betrayed, and mistreated, but I am here to tell you that that is a lie. And I want to encourage you to find your tribe. Learn to trust and learn to forgive others quickly because forgiveness is not for them, it's for you. And let me be clear, just because you forgive them doesn't mean that they must have access to you anymore. Learn to take control of how much you give to people. I'm learning when I meet people to ask, "What's my assignment in your life?" I learned that from Apostle Mark. He also said that you are not worth my favor! That helps me act accordingly in my response to people. I must remember that everyone is battling something and there may be something about me that resembles that area of their life. I've learned to pray for people instead of judging them.

Just remember this, God is an intentional God and He wants the best for us because we are his children.

# GOD'S PROMISES TO YOU

I tell you most of my life story to tell you that God is always there, no matter what. Even when you sin, God is there and He's waiting on you. He doesn't care about what you did, He cares about where you're going. So, ask Him for forgiveness, repent (that means to turn from your evil ways), and forgive yourself. It's that simple. I'm not saying that it's going to be easy to do either part, but it's that simple to be redeemed. The question is are you willing to put in the work? Becoming the best version of yourself is work! Work that doesn't always feel good, but it's worth it. The more work I put in the better I feel, the lighter I feel. Don't get me wrong, I am far from perfect. But I am not who I used to be, and I give all the glory to God. The times I wanted to take my life; He kept me. He kept me so I could look back over my life and see where He's brought me from.

When I really reflect over my life and how God kept me, my eyes fill with tears. Not tears of sorrow, but tears of joy! I cry because I think of all the years I could have been dead by my own hands. I think about all the things I could have missed, and it reminds me that I was selfish. I would have missed my sons growing up and I wouldn't have been able to watch them become who they are. All three of my sons graduated from high school, two with honors. I have been blessed to watch them become productive citizens of this world. I would have never seen the birth of my beautiful baby girl, and experience how she helped change my life. I can honestly say she helped mold and change me and alter some of my behaviors. I could have missed being there for my mom when we thought we were going to lose my stepdad. I could have missed saying "I do" for the first time and all the life experiences that came along with that. I would have missed all the lives I touched by telling my story.

See, what I have come to realize is all the stuff we go through in life isn't for us, it's for us to help someone else. It's for us to tell our own story and not have it written in our obituary. In this life, we are going to have some ups, downs, ins, outs, good times, and bad days. Yet, when you sit and look back over your life, you will find God's Glory, and say that it was all worth it. You see God is waiting for you. You don't have to get right and then go to God. Go to God and He will get you right. He has a plan for you. He created you before the foundation of the earth. He has a purpose with your name on it and although it may look like someone else's plan, I promise yours is customized for you; it's God designed. Don't forfeit what God has for you because of your own agenda. I can tell you that my worst days with God are better than my best days without Him.

I don't know if anyone has told you this lately, but God loves you and so do I. Go on with your life and be great!